DECODING LEADERSHIP

DECODING LEADERSHIP

THE DYNAMICS OF FASCISM, DEMOCRACY AND TECHNOCRACY

Marco Tavanti, PhD

Decoding Leadership: The Dynamics of Fascism, Democracy, and Technocracy
Copyright © 2025 Marco Tavanti, PhD

All rights reserved. No part of this book may be reproduced, stored in a retrieval system, or transmitted in any form or by any means—electronic, mechanical, photocopying, recording, or otherwise—without prior written permission from the publisher, except for brief quotations in reviews or academic references.

Published by
Bene Comune Press
San Francisco, CA

ISBN: 979-8-9922083-0-6 (Print-Softcover)
ISBN: 979-8-9922083-1-3 (e-Book)
LCCN: 2025904833 (Library of Congress Control Number)

First Edition: 2025

Printed in the United States of America
Published on May 8, 2025, commemorating the 80th anniversary of the Nazi surrender in World War II.

Bene Comune Press is dedicated to publishing works that advance critical education, leadership, and the common good. For more information, visit https://benecomunepress.com.
For permissions, inquiries, or bulk orders, contact benecomunepress@mail.com

This book is printed using Print-on-Demand (POD) technology, which supports sustainability by reducing waste, minimizing overproduction, and lowering the carbon footprint associated with traditional publishing methods.

Disclaimer: This book represents the views and research of the author. While every effort has been made to ensure accuracy, the publisher and author assume no responsibility for errors, omissions, or any consequences from the application of information in this book.

*Al mio babbo Primo
and my father-in-law Marty*

CONTENTS

List of Tables	ix
Foreword	xi
Preface	xiii
Introduction	xix
Part I: Decoding Governance Dynamics	1
Chapter 1. Decoding Leadership Powers	3
The Power of Service	9
The Power of Responsibility	11
The Power of Care	13
Leadership as People Power	15
Leadership as Moral Intelligence	19
Chapter 2. Decoding the Governance Spectrum	23
Additional Governance Typologies	25
Comparing the Governance Spectrum	30
Dynamics Across Governance Models	33
Leadership Across Government Types	36
Ecosystemic Lenses on Governance	40
Chapter 3. Decoding Governance Transformations	43
How Governance Evolves and Leaders Emerge	45
Discontent Movements and Change Leaders	49
Leaders Advancing-Receding Governance Progress	55
Why Leaders Should Promote Evolution	61
Governance as Dynamic System	69

Part II: Decoding Fascist Dynamics   73
Chapter 4. Decoding Fascism   75
    The Recurrent Nature of Authoritarianism   81
    Fascist Dynamics in the 21st Century   87
    Fascist Leadership: The Cult of The Strongman   92
    Fascism and the Manipulation of Information   94
    Understanding Fascism as a Mindset   99
    Fascist Leadership as Concentration of Power   106
    The American Fascist Paradox   107
Chapter 5. Decoding Anti-Fascism   113
    Anti-Fascism and Economic Justice   119
    Anti-Fascism and Critical Education   124
    Anti-Fascism and Liberating Religion   133
    Countering Fascism   138
Chapter 6. Decoding Techno-Fascism   143
    Oligarchs for Algorithmic Governance   147
    Techno-Democracy vs. Techno-Fascism   150
    Technological Governance for Democratic Future   155
    Ethics And Education for Techno-Democracy   158
Epilogue   161
References   167
Appendix 1: Glossary   183
Appendix 2: Annotated Bibliography   191
Appendix 3: GCQ Assessment   197
Appendix 4: ARI Assessment   201
Index   205
About the Author   209

LIST OF TABLES

Table 1.1: Leadership Power Dynamics	7
Table 1.2: Resistance to Political Leadership	17
Table 2.1: Governance Typologies and Dynamics	34
Table 3.1: Governance and Leadership Factors	48
Table 3.2: Social Movements and Change Leadership	52
Table 3.3: Leaders' Response to Events	59
Table 3.4: Government and Business Leadership Dynamics	67
Table 4.1: Comparing Mussolini's Fascism with Other Systems	79
Table 4.2: Fascist Dynamics in Authoritarian Leaders	97
Table 4.3: Fascist and Anti-Fascist Mindsets	101
Table 5.1: Anti-Fascist Leaders' Contributions	115
Table 5.2: Fascist vs. Post-Fascist Economic Systems	121
Table 5.3: Critical Anti-Fascist Education	125
Table 5.4: Anti-Fascist Mindsets in Education	132
Table 5.5: Anti-Fascist Religious Mindsets	137
Table 6.1: Techno-Fascism Related Terms	145
Table 6.2: Technology & Governance Outcomes	152

FOREWORD

Leadership is not merely about holding power—it is about shaping the destiny of nations and the well-being of future generations. In Chile, my country, we have lived through the darkest consequences of authoritarian rule, as well as the hope that democracy and justice can bring. We have seen what it means to govern through fear, and we have seen what it means to lead with solidarity. Today, as we stand at a crossroads, where the future of our planet and our people is at stake, we must ask ourselves: What kind of leadership do we need? What kind of leadership do we deserve?

For too long, history has been marked by leaders who prioritized control over collaboration, profit over people, and power over principle. Thus, governance, politics, economics and business are often practiced within an ethical and moral vacuum. The dictatorship of Augusto Pinochet left deep wounds in Chile, not only through its repression and violence but through an economic system that fueled inequality and environmental degradation. His leadership was built on the false premise that order justifies oppression, that development excuses exploitation. We must reject this model.

Instead, we must look to leaders who choose a path of democracy, social justice, and human dignity. Leaders who understand that true leadership is not about imposing authority but about empowering others. Leaders who demonstrate that sustainable development, gender equality, and human rights are not obstacles to progress, but its foundation.

As a candidate for the Chilean Green Party, I have long advocated for leadership that serves both people and the planet. We need leaders who understand that democracy and sustainability go hand in hand, that economic prosperity must be shared, and that ecological responsibility is not a choice but an obligation. We need leaders who will not just do good, but who will be good—who will embody the values of peace, justice, and respect for all forms of life.

As the United Nations approaches its 80th anniversary, we must reflect on its founding vision: the pursuit of global peace. This vision is not an abstract ideal but a necessary path forward. True peace is not merely the absence of war—it is the presence of justice, equality, and sustainability. It is about ensuring that future generations inherit a world where they can thrive, not struggle against the consequences of our failures.

We owe this commitment not only to those who came before us—who fought for democracy, for human rights, for the preservation of our planet—but to those who will come after us. The next generation deserves a world shaped by wisdom, not greed; by cooperation, not domination. They deserve leaders who understand that the greatest power one can wield is the ability to inspire others toward goodness.

This book, *Decoding Leadership: The Dynamics of Fascism, Democracy, and Technocracy*, offers an opportunity to reflect on the kind of leadership that will define our future. May it serve as a reminder that the choices we make today will determine the world of tomorrow. Let us choose wisely. Let us choose peace. Let us choose democracy. Let us choose sustainability for our common future.

Dr. Alfredo Sfeir-Younis
Former Presidential Candidate, Chilean Green Party

PREFACE

"The old world is dying, and the new world struggles to be born: Now is the time of monsters."

— Antonio Gramsci, 1929

To resist fascism, we must first understand it. Anti-fascism is not just about opposing tyranny—it is about cultivating ethical leadership, reinforcing democratic institutions, and ensuring democracy is not just preserved but continuously renewed. Hemingway (1940) wrote in *For Whom the Bell Tolls*, "Are you a communist?" "No, I am an anti-fascist." "For a long time?" "Since I have understood fascism." This is the kind of clarity we urgently need today. I wrote this book to deepen that understanding—and to help future generations learn how to recognize and stop fascism before it takes root.

Education plays a central role in this struggle. Fascist and corporate systems thrive on conformity, suppressing critical thinking, and discouraging active civic engagement. Pink Floyd's song "Another Brick in the Wall" offers a powerful critique of authoritarian educational models, where students are treated as passive recipients of knowledge rather than as individuals capable of questioning the world around them. The chorus— "We don't need no education. We don't need no thought control."—is not a rejection of education but a rebellion against oppressive systems that condition people to accept authority without question. An anti-fascist education, by contrast, encourages critical thought, diversity of perspectives, and the courage to challenge oppressive structures.

As Don Lorenzo Milani, an anti-fascist Catholic priest and educator from Florence, Italy, famously stated, "A school that is neutral does not exist. The school is either a place of liberation or it is an instrument of oppression" (Milani, 1967, p. 12). He also warned against the dangers of political apathy, recognizing that in times of injustice, neutrality often aligns with oppression, *"Ventotto apolitici e tre fascisti uguale a trentuno fascisti"* (Twenty-eight apolitical people and three fascists make thirty-one fascists) (Milani, 1967, p. 45). In other words, silence and inaction in the face of authoritarianism enable its spread, reinforcing the need for an education that does not shy away from confronting power but actively works to dismantle structures of oppression.

This book examines how fascism mutates and adapts—how it disguises itself under the language of democracy, economic stability, and even technological progress. One of the most pressing concerns of our time is the rise of technocratic governance, where policy is increasingly determined not by democratic debate but by experts, algorithms, and artificial intelligence. While technocracy presents itself as a rational alternative to partisan politics, it also raises urgent questions about accountability, legitimacy, and the erosion of public participation. What happens when unelected corporate executives have more influence over government policy than elected representatives? What happens when, as studies from the Massachusetts Institute of Technology (MIT) have shown, the overuse of artificial intelligence diminishes analytical thinking and critical reasoning, leading to a passive acceptance of AI-driven decisions without scrutiny, thereby eroding democratic participation and creating an unaccountable technocratic authority (Rahwan et al., 2019)?

This book emerges from my students' questions, "Why do people tend to follow fascist leaders?" "Why is there such a fascination with strongman leadership?" "Why aren't we in the streets protesting as governments and corporations systematically erode our basic rights?" Writing this book is my attempt to understand these questions.

The world is undergoing profound transformations, where governance, leadership, and power structures are shifting in ways that often defy traditional categories. Democracy is under siege, corporate influence has expanded beyond the control of elected governments, authoritarian populism continues to rise, and technocracy is increasingly shaping public policy. Yet, amid these upheavals, one of the greatest dangers is the tendency to overgeneralize—to assume that all systems of power operate in the same way, that leadership is either inherently authoritarian or democratic, or that anti-fascist resistance necessarily leads to just governance.

The Italian saying *"Fare di tutta l'erba un fascio"*—to make a bundle out of all the herbs—cautions against being careless. There's a tendency for this to happen when we discuss politics, power, or leadership. Words like "fascism" or "democracy" get tossed around without much thought. For me, fascism was always a vague idea—something from old history books or grainy documentaries. I grew up in Italy, where the term has deep roots, but I never felt I fully understood it. Moving to the United States, I started to notice familiar patterns in new forms—rhetoric, control, fear. I wrote this book to better understand what these words mean for us today, and how they shape the world we live in.

Educational institutions have a key responsibility to provide the necessary critical capacity to discern the forces of power and the moral, human, and systemic consequences. Fascism is not an outdated phenomenon, a relic of World War II confined to the history books. It is a political tool that re-emerges whenever societies become disillusioned, institutions weaken, and fear is manipulated for political gain. As Antonio Gramsci (1971) noted, fascism does not emerge as a conventional ideology but rather as an anti-party movement—one that feeds on chaos, resentment, and the manipulation of mass psychology. It offers deceptively simple answers to complex problems, cloaking its true intentions in vague rhetoric and a rejection of established political norms. This characterization resonates with the liberal translation of Gramsci—popularized by Slavoj Žižek (2010)—that opens this preface, "Now is the time of monsters," a vivid rendering of Gramsci's original observation, "In this interregnum a great variety of morbid symptoms appear." The enduring relevance of this warning is echoed by Sandro Pertini, one of Italy's most respected political leaders, who captured the essence of the threat when he declared, "All ideas must be respected, except fascism. Fascism is not an idea; it is the death of all ideas" (Pertini, 1973, p. 34).

This is the fundamental truth that modern political discourse often ignores. Fascism is not just another political belief—it is a system that, by its very nature, eradicates all other beliefs. It thrives on obedience, uniformity, and the suppression of critical thought. Pier Paolo Pasolini, in his analysis of post-war Italy, argued that a new form of fascism had emerged—not through military control, but through consumer culture, economic coercion, and the subtle imposition of conformity (Pasolini, 1975). This form of fascism does not march in the streets or wear uniforms; instead, it manifests through the consolidation of corporate power, the monopolization of public discourse, and the transformation of citizens into passive consumers rather than active participants in democracy.

In this light, Mussolini's doctrine promoted a corporative system in which divergent social and economic interests were coordinated and subordinated to the unity of the State (Mussolini, 1935). While the popular quote, "Fascism should more appropriately be called Corporatism because it is a merger of state and corporate power," is often misattributed or inaccurately translated, it effectively captures the essence of Mussolini's vision. As he stated, "The corporate State considers that private enterprise in the sphere of production is the most effective and useful instrument in the interest of the nation" (p. 135). This fusion of political and economic power under authoritarian control remains a defining characteristic of fascist economic structures.

Today, corporate power has become so entrenched in governance that private interests now wield influence far beyond that of ordinary citizens. President Franklin D. Roosevelt warned of this danger when he said, "The liberty of a democracy is not safe if the people tolerate the growth of private power to a point where it becomes stronger than their democratic state itself. That, in its essence, is fascism—ownership of government by an individual, by a group, or by any other controlling private power." (Roosevelt, 1938).

The danger is not just outright authoritarianism, but the slow erosion of democracy under the guise of efficiency and expertise. As Noam Chomsky (2010) warned, "The United States is extremely lucky that no honest, charismatic figure has arisen. Every charismatic figure is such an obvious crook that he destroys himself, like McCarthy or Nixon or the evangelist preachers. If somebody comes along who is charismatic and honest, this country is in real trouble because of the frustration, disillusionment, the justified anger, and the absence of any coherent response." The threat is not just dictatorship in its traditional form but the rise of a system in which democracy exists in name only—where elections still happen, but real power lies elsewhere.

George Orwell (1949) famously stated in his book *Nineteen Eighty-Four*, "In a time of universal deceit, telling the truth is a revolutionary act." His book is an attempt to tell the truth—not just about fascism, but about the systems that allow it to take root. It is an attempt to move beyond historical nostalgia and recognize the realities of power in the 21st century. The struggle is not merely to prevent fascism from returning in its old forms but to understand how it operates today, under different names and within different institutions. The question we must ask ourselves is not just how to resist fascism, but how to build a world where fascism can never take root again.

This is our task. Let's begin!

INTRODUCTION

"I greet with wonderful energy the American people and I see and recognize among you the salt of your land, as well as ours, my fellow citizens who are working to make America great."

— Benito Mussolini, 1927

Fascism and anti-fascism are deeply personal to me. They have shaped my family's history on both the American side and the Italian side. My dear father-in-law, Private Marty, fought in World War II, landing on Omaha Beach with the 2nd Rangers Special Force Unit, Company C, as depicted in Steven Spielberg's movie *Saving Private Ryan* (1998). The character played by Tom Hanks, Captain Ralph Goranson, was Marty's own commanding officer, who was also from Chicago. My wife and I have retraced his steps across Europe, following military records and historical accounts, documenting his heroic resistance alongside the many courageous soldiers of the Greatest Generation who fought against Nazi tyranny.

Even during his time, this ideological fight was not as clear-cut as history often portrays. While Marty risked his life to defeat the Nazis, many Americans sympathized with fascist ideology. Charles Lindbergh, for example, openly supported Hitler's expansionism before the war, and groups like the German American Bund organized pro-Nazi rallies on American soil (Bennett, 2018). Even within Marty's own family, divisions existed—his own cousin traveled back to Europe and chose to fight on the side of the Nazis in Italy, reflecting the painful reality that fascism's appeal was not confined to any single nation.

Our research carefully documented the battles from Normandy to Brest, the liberation of Paris, and the brutal combat in the Hürtgen Forest and Hill 400, where Marty was wounded. He lost many dear friends, like Doc Roberts, before heading to the Battle of the Bulge, where he and his unit played a critical role in rescuing surrounded American forces. Eventually, he was part of the liberation of concentration camps, an experience that left an indelible mark on him. Because of their heroic service, the "Band of Brothers", as they were later called, were dismissed without being redeployed to the ongoing war in the Pacific (Ambrose, 1992).

Through this research, we uncovered a history of bravery and essential lessons in leadership and adaptability. For example, the Rangers were trained to be nimble and quickly adapt to unexpected circumstances, such as scaling Pointe du Hoc and Pointe de la Percée during D-Day, without waiting for orders from the chain of command (Atkinson, 2002). We also conducted this research to share these stories with Marty's grandchildren, ensuring they understood the sacrifices that secured peace and prosperity for the last 80 years.

Yet, after the war, Marty did not define himself by heroism or medals. He focused on family, love, and hard work while also dedicating himself to a quieter form of leadership. He became one of the first coaches of an inclusive Little League baseball team in Maywood, Illinois, where white middle-class kids played alongside African American, Native American, and Latino immigrant children—an uncommon sight in 1950s America. A time when racial integration was still widely resisted (Sugrue, 2008). Meanwhile, his wife, Nancy, became an advocate for disability rights, inspired by their daughter Mary, who lived with disabilities. Her work led her to collaborate with African American leaders in the Civil Rights Movement, including Fred Hampton, the influential Chicago organizer of the Black Panther Party, who famously advocated for interracial solidarity against oppression (Rhodes, 2007).

While my father-in-law fought fascism on the battlefield, my Italian family endured it inside their own homes. They experienced firsthand the brutality of Nazi-Fascist repression, the courageous resistance of the *Partigiani* (partisan fighters) and the horrors of World War II.

On my mother's side, my family experienced the Massacre of Civitella in Val di Chiana, a Nazi retaliation on June 29, 1944, in which 244 innocent civilians were executed, including my great-grandfather Carlo (Battini, 2014). The massacre was one of many in Tuscany, carried out as retribution for Partigiani resistance activity. In Civitella, Nazi forces systematically executed men, women, and children, attempting to crush the growing opposition to fascist rule (Baldini & Cavallaro, 2010).

On my father's side, tragedy struck in Manciano della Chiana on April 24, 1944, when an erroneous Allied airstrike intended to destroy a nearby railway bridge missed its target and instead hit my family's home, killing four adults and two children, including my great-grandfather, Francesco. The loss was devastating, and while an official apology letter and monetary compensation were eventually received, no amount of reparation money could erase the pain of losing family members in such a tragic and unintended way (Eatwell, 2011).

A few years ago, we conducted research into these events, accessing U.S. military records with the assistance of a retired U.S. Air Force general. These documents provided new insights into the tactical decisions that led to the airstrike errors, but even more revealing was the testimony of an eyewitness family friend who was there that day. He also described the stark humanity on all sides of the conflict. As farmers, they fed whoever was hungry—whether young German soldiers or the young *Partigiani* in desperate need of food. The reality of war was far more complex than simple divisions of "good" and "evil"—suffering was everywhere, and acts of compassion coexisted with the horrors of war (Klinkhammer, 1993).

One side of my family strongly identified with the Catholic Church, partly because my grandfather Santi was a *mezzadro* (sharecropper), living in quasi-indentured servitude to Cardinal Giovanni Battista Montini, who later became Pope Paul VI. My father vividly recalled how the future pope, during his travels between Milan and Rome, would stop at their farm, play with the children, and enjoy simple meals made from fresh farm ingredients. Their deep devotion to the Catholic Church remained, and as Pope Paul VI, Montini later took a firm stance against Fascism and the Nazi regime, recognizing the need for a Church that stood for justice rather than political power (Hebblethwaite, 1993).

Interestingly, my ancestors also played a role in economic and social development in Tuscany. My family worked as farmers in the Val di Chiana, a region that benefited from extensive land reclamation projects (*bonifiche*), sometimes erroneously attributed to Benito Mussoli who took credit for the work of others (Alexander, 1984). Some of these economic policies were coordinated by Benedetto Tavanti, the brother of Judge Angiolo Tavanti, an ancestor of mine. Judge Tavanti became a prominent figure in the Grand Duchy of Tuscany under Holy Roman Emperor Leopold II, where he implemented taxation reforms (*Catasto*) for fairer land ownership designations and eliminated trade barriers (*dazi*) to promote commercial exchange (Pellegrini, 2008). Though largely unknown today, Judge Angiolo Tavanti left a lasting legacy in economic justice and governance, and his remains lie in Santa Croce, Florence, alongside Galileo Galilei, Michelangelo, and Machiavelli—a testament to his influence during a time of profound political and economic transformation.

These family histories—of resistance and suffering, faith and survival, leadership and reform—reflect the complex realities of fascism and its aftermath. The lessons we take from them are not just personal but universal: History is shaped not only by political ideology but also by human choices, and it is these choices that define whether societies succumb to oppression or fight for justice and dignity.

My understanding of these lessons deepened through my academic and professional journey, beginning with the insights of Professor Enrico Chiavacci, a renowned moral theologian who taught social ethics from an anti-fascist standpoint. I vividly remember my final oral exam with him in Florence, where he posed the same question to every student, "What is the definition of the principle of subsidiarity?" At the time, I did not fully understand the significance of his method of teaching. Only later did I realize that his insistence on this one question was a deliberate effort to challenge authoritarian thinking and ensure that we understood how the Nazi-Fascist model of imposed centralization directly contradicted Catholic Social Teaching's core principle of subsidiarity (Chiavacci, 2001).

Subsidiarity, is a principle that advocates for decision-making at the most local and competent level possible. It serves as a safeguard against the overreach of state power. Jacques Maritain, one of the most influential Catholic philosophers of the 20th century and a key figure in shaping modern democratic humanism, argued that "The principle of subsidiarity is opposed to all the abuses of state power; it represents the right of communities to settle their own affairs as much as possible" (Tavanti & Wilp, 2021, p. 249). This perspective greatly influenced Professor Chiavacci, Pope Paul VI, and many of the Catholic intellectuals who resisted fascist ideologies.

During my studies and work in Florence, I had the honor of learning from conscientious objectors such as Padre Ernesto Balducci, who viewed war as the ultimate failure of human civilization, and Mayor Giorgio La Pira, who championed social justice, peace, and urban renewal as resistance to fascism and the promotion of democratic participation. I was also profoundly influenced by the teachings of Don Lorenzo Milani, whose strong commitment to educational justice and the empowerment of the poor stood in direct opposition to the elitism and exclusionary policies of fascism (Milani, 1967).

Later, my international experiences—working with communities across Africa and Latin America—helped me understand the global struggles for social justice, human rights, and labor rights. Through these experiences, I began to see more clearly why people around the world sought better opportunities and the recognition of their fundamental rights. Yet, one question continued to trouble me, why were so many working-class people in Italy still supporting Silvio Berlusconi, despite his neoliberal policies that did so little to benefit them?

In Chiapas, Mexico, I learned from the Maya Indigenous communities, particularly from *Las Abejas*, a Christian pacifist group dedicated to social justice and Indigenous rights (Tavanti, 2003). Their struggle was deeply connected to with the legacy of Bishop Samuel Ruiz García, who followed in the footsteps of Fray Bartolomé de las Casas, advocating for Indigenous self-determination, human dignity, and liberation theology (Camayd-Freixas, 2008). The Zapatista movement and its sympathizers rejected economic models imposed upon them—models symbolized by the neoliberal agenda of NAFTA, which promoted free trade and development while systematically excluding the voices and alternative values of Indigenous communities and their ecosystems (Harvey, 1998). These resistance movements have played a crucial role in opposing political and economic structures of repression and advocating for the inclusion of historically marginalized populations.

My later work in collaboration with various leaders, agencies, and programs at the United Nations (UN) further broadened my understanding of how international cooperation can serve as a bulwark against authoritarianism and conflict. The United Nations, conceived from the vision of President Franklin D. Roosevelt (FDR) and officially established in San Francisco in 1945, represents the most comprehensive global investment in peace, democracy, and the rule of law. Its Charter articulates the commitment to preventing future world wars and fostering development and humanitarian assistance, ensuring that nations have the human, economic, and political conditions necessary for lasting peace and prosperity (United Nations, 1945). As FDR envisioned, the UN remains an indispensable institution for defending human dignity and freedom, particularly for the peoples of the world living under oppression. His words echo today as a reminder of what is at stake, "The structure of world peace cannot be the work of one man, or one party, or one nation... It must be a peace which rests on the cooperative effort of the whole world" (Roosevelt, 1945). The UN, despite its challenges, continues to serve as a platform for global cooperation, ensuring that the lessons of fascism's destruction and the resistance against it are not forgotten. Through its work in peacekeeping, human rights advocacy, and sustainable development, the UN embodies the collective aspirations of nations and peoples to live "in larger freedom", as stated in its foundational documents (United Nations, 2005).

The struggle against fascism, authoritarianism, and systemic oppression is far from over. Whether in the trenches of World War II, the resistance movements of Latin America and Africa, or the international diplomacy of the United Nations, the fight for human dignity, justice, and self-determination continues to define our era. As history has shown, fascism thrives in apathy and complacency, while democracy and justice require active engagement.

This book is my attempt to decode the dynamics of power, resistance, and leadership, not only through historical and political analysis but through the lived experiences of those who have fought for justice across generations. The lessons I have learned—from my family's sacrifices, my mentors' teachings, and the struggles of communities worldwide—serve as both a warning and a call to action:

We must never remain neutral in the face of oppression.

We also must recognize our responsibility to be educated about the past and present dynamics of fascism and anti-fascism. Following the second election of President Trump in the United States, social media was flooded with questions about why so many people would support an authoritarian leader. I recall reading a post that said something like:

We taught an entire generation that fascism was bad… but we didn't explain why.

This resonated with my own educational experience in Italy, where I studied the histories of the Egyptians and Romans in great detail but learned relatively little about World War II and the modern global order. While curriculum requirements may be partly to blame, Don Lorenzo Milani, in *Letter to a Teacher,* exposed a deeper issue: Our education system often avoids teaching about fascism and other politically sensitive contemporary realities:

> You [teacher], with your Greeks and your Romans, had made him [Gianni, the poor student] hate history. But we, going through the Second World War, could hold him for hours without a break. [...] One woman teacher ended her lessons before the First World War. She stopped exactly at the spot where school could tie us to life. In the whole year she never once read a newspaper to her class. The Fascist posters must still be dangling before her eyes: 'Do not talk politics in here.' (Milani & Barbiana School, 2004).

This book aims to equip my students and future generations with the tools to critically analyze and navigate contemporary political dynamics by examining historical events that remain highly relevant today. It seeks to foster critical thinking and a transdisciplinary mindset by encouraging the differentiation, comparison, and contrast of leadership examples, power dynamics, and governance patterns. Divided into two parts, the book is designed to deepen our understanding of leadership and governance in the face of rising authoritarianism.

Part 1: Decoding Governance Dynamics examines governance as a dynamic system, exploring how leadership structures have shaped societies throughout history and continue to do so today. Leadership and governance models are influenced by cultural, political, and economic contexts, making it essential to move beyond simplistic binaries such as democracy versus fascism or good versus evil. Instead, we apply ethical, social, political, and economic frameworks to analyze power structures and their influence on national, corporate, and global stability. This section introduces the core leadership powers—service, responsibility, and care—as fundamental to ethical governance. We also investigate how governance systems evolve, why leaders rise, and how movements of discontent drive systemic change.

Part 2: Decoding Fascism Dynamics takes a focused look at the mechanics of authoritarian power, dissecting the rise of fascist ideologies and their modern manifestations. We will examine the cult of the strongman, propaganda tactics, and the erosion of democratic norms, highlighting patterns that enable authoritarian control. Importantly, this section is not just about diagnosis—it also explores resistance. By understanding historical antifascist movements, economic justice strategies, critical education initiatives, and the role of liberating religious movements, we can identify pathways to fostering democratic, participatory, and accountable leadership. We will also analyze techno-fascism, techno-populism, and the interconnection of modern technologies with authoritarian leadership governance dynamics.

Throughout the book, comparative tables serve as a vital tool for reflecting on leadership values and practices, drawing from historical lessons and contemporary case studies. These structured comparisons invite us to analyze patterns of governance, ethical dilemmas, and the impact of leadership decisions across different historical and political contexts. By examining both authoritarian and democratic leadership models side by side, we can better understand the underlying forces that shape governance, the warning signs of authoritarianism, and the transformative potential of ethical (principled) leadership (Tavanti, 2023).

This approach equips us with the historical insight, ethical discernment, and strategic action necessary to challenge authoritarian tendencies. It encourages us to recognize the responsibilities that come with leadership and the ways in which power can be wielded either for oppression or for the common good. By developing a nuanced understanding of governance, we can advocate for systems that uphold justice, integrity, and accountability—ensuring that power serves all people, not just the privileged few.

PART I
DECODING GOVERNANCE DYNAMICS

| 1 |

DECODING LEADERSHIP POWERS

"Power tends to corrupt, and absolute power corrupts absolutely. Great men are almost always bad men, even when they exercise influence and not authority: still more when you super add the tendency or the certainty of corruption by authority."

— Lord Acton, 1887

Leadership is a force that has shaped civilizations across history, influencing governance, economies, and institutions. While the world has evolved, the fundamental nature of leadership remains constant. We know that the struggles for power, authority, and legitimacy that once defined rulers and revolutionaries continue to shape societies today.

Corruption is a common characteristic, unfortunately, observed in too many examples of leadership, both in historical and contemporary practices. Yet, corruption is not simply a result of unethical personal leadership choices but a complex dynamic resulting from unchecked powers and unaccountable or ineffective mechanisms for checks and balances. Ethical practices are one of the many responsibility factors that explain corrupt and toxic leadership behaviors in organizations and societal governance.

Building on Patrick Lencioni's (2002) *The Five Dysfunctions of a Team*, I have spent the past 20+ years working with leaders across sectors and around the world, observing patterns of behavior that undermine ethical and effective leadership. From this experience, I have identified what I call *The Five Dynamics of Corrupt Leadership*—a framework that highlights how corruption emerges, takes root, and persists within leadership structures. While terminology may vary across leadership ethics and organizational behavior literature, these five dynamics offer a widely observable pattern that cuts across business, government, and nonprofit sectors. They are described as follows:

1. **Abuse of Power:** Corrupt leaders often exploit their position for personal gain, using their authority to bypass rules, silence opposition, or enrich themselves or their allies. This includes favoritism, nepotism, and coercion.

2. **Lack of Accountability:** When checks and balances are weak or ignored, corrupt leaders operate with impunity. A lack of transparency and oversight enables misconduct to flourish unchallenged.

3. **Culture of Fear or Silence:** Corrupt leadership often maintains control by fostering a culture where dissent is punished, whistleblowers are marginalized, and ethical concerns are dismissed or suppressed.

4. **Normalization of Deviance:** Over time, unethical behavior becomes routine and even expected. Minor infractions escalate, and what once was considered corrupt becomes seen as just "how things are done around here."

5. **Complicity and Enablers:** Corrupt leaders rarely act alone. They are often supported by a network of enablers—advisors,

subordinates, or institutions—who benefit from the system and help cover up wrongdoing.

Ethical leadership is about acting righteously, even in the face of powerful pressures to do otherwise. As I once learned from a military leader who stood firm on his principles—and paid a steep career price for speaking truth to power—true ethical leadership goes beyond doing the right thing when no one is watching. As he put it, "Ethical leadership is not just about doing the right thing when people aren't watching. It's about doing the right thing when people *are* watching—and when they want you to do the opposite" (Tavanti & Stachowicz-Stanusch, 2014).

In my Ethical Leadership courses, I regularly engage graduate students in the analysis of real-world cases of leadership corruption—many of which have led to scandals and legal consequences across various sectors. Together, we have developed a curated collection of cases and case studies, which are integrated into the curriculum to foster moral intelligence and strengthen ethical decision-making. The goal is to prepare students to navigate the complexity and pressures of real-world power dynamics with integrity and courage (Tavanti, 2022).

These "five dynamics" explain how corruption manifests similarly across business, political, and nonprofit sectors. Often, it begins with an abuse of power, such as a CEO awarding contracts to friends, a politician diverting public funds for personal campaigns, or a nonprofit leader prioritizing personal alliances over mission-based decisions. This misuse of authority is sustained by a lack of accountability, where boards, oversight agencies, or governance structures fail to enforce checks and balances—be it a corporate board overlooking unethical practices, a government disbanding a watchdog institution, or a nonprofit with weak financial controls.

A culture of fear or silence further entrenches corruption, as whistleblowers in corporations face retaliation, journalists in authoritarian regimes are silenced, and nonprofit staff risk losing their jobs for questioning leadership. Over time, these behaviors become routine, leading to a normalization of deviance where unethical conduct is no longer seen as wrong—whether it is bribery becoming standard in business deals, false reporting in nonprofits, or routine graft in government. Finally, corrupt leaders rarely act alone; they rely on a network of complicity and enablers—advisors, auditors, donors, or political allies—who benefit from the system and choose to ignore wrongdoing. Together, these dynamics create environments where corruption not only survives but thrives across sectors.

Numerous studies tell us that leadership is not merely the act of holding power but the ethical responsibility of wielding it for the collective good. As Burns (1978) famously observed, "Leadership is one of the most observed and least understood phenomena on earth" (p. 2). Throughout history—from emperors and statesmen to revolutionaries and activists—leaders have grappled with the same enduring questions, how is power obtained? How should it be exercised? And what moral obligations accompany it?

Power in leadership is a double-edged sword—it can be a catalyst for progress or a tool of oppression. When used ethically, it has the power to inspire, uplift communities, and drive meaningful social change. Leaders committed to the common good leverage their influence to promote equity, sustainability, and justice. However, history is equally replete with instances where power has been wielded for personal gain, corruption, and tyranny.

Lord Acton, one of the great personalities of the 19th century, beside his well-known warning on power and corruption also said that "Despotic power is always accompanied by corruption of morality [...] Authority that does not exist for Liberty is not authority but force [...] Absolute power demoralizes" (Acton Institute). This underscores the critical need for accountability, ethical leadership, and institutional checks that prevent the descent into authoritarianism.

The quote, "Nearly all men can stand adversity, but if you want to test a man's character, give him power," often attributed to President Abraham Lincoln but likely originating from Illinois Attorney General Robert G. Ingersoll, highlights a fundamental truth: True leadership is not merely about holding authority but about the integrity and ethical responsibility that comes with it. Max Weber's (1947) concept of "legitimate authority" provides a useful framework for understanding leadership, distinguishing between traditional, charismatic, and bureaucratic leadership structures. However, legitimacy alone does not determine the true value of leadership—what ultimately matters is how power is exercised and whose interests it serves.

Table 1.1: Leadership Power Dynamics

LEADERSHIP POWER	BALANCED LEADERSHIP VS. EXTREMES
POWER OF SERVICE	Balance: Ethical stewardship, humility. Deficiency: Neglecting duty, self-interest. Excess: Burnout, enabling dependency.
POWER OF RESPONSIBILITY	Balance: Integrity, transparency. Deficiency: Avoiding accountability, blaming others. Excess: Micromanaging, over-controlling.
POWER OF CARE	Balance: Empathy, inclusivity. Deficiency: Indifference, emotional detachment. Excess: Over-sentimentality, enabling harm.
POWER OF INFLUENCE	Balance: Inspiring positive change. Deficiency: Passivity, lack of motivation. Excess: Manipulation, coercion.
POWER OF DECISION-MAKING	Balance: Ethical, strategic choices. Deficiency: Indecisiveness, lack of vision. Excess: Authoritarianism, recklessness.
POWER OF COMMUNICATION	Balance: Clear, truthful dialogue. Deficiency: Poor clarity, miscommunication. Excess: Excessive rhetoric, manipulation.
POWER OF INNOVATION	Balance: Creativity, responsible progress. Deficiency: Resistance to change, stagnation. Excess: Chaotic disruption, reckless experiments.

To navigate the complexities of leadership power, it is essential to understand its three dimensions: Deficiency, balanced virtue, and excess. The essence of ethical leadership lies in striking a balance—where power is neither neglected nor abused. A lack of authority leads to weak governance and disorder, while excessive control breeds oppression and authoritarianism.

The exercise of leadership power exists along a spectrum—from its virtuous application to harmful distortions driven by excess or deficiency. Understanding this dynamic is crucial for developing ethical and effective leaders. Table 1.1 illustrates this spectrum, highlighting how leadership virtues, when exercised with integrity, can uphold justice and serve the common good, whereas extremes of deficiency or excess lead to dysfunction and harm. This framework encourages reflection on the ethical use of power and the importance of balance in cultivating responsible leadership.

Throughout history, leaders have wielded power in strikingly different ways. Some have used their influence to advance the common good, strengthen institutions, and promote justice, while others have sought to consolidate personal control, suppress dissent, or exploit resources for self-serving or political ends. As leadership structures and models evolve, the core questions remain unchanged: How is power acquired, exercised, and sustained? More importantly, how does leadership contribute to the well-being of individuals and society? The legitimacy of leadership is not measured solely by its ability to command but by its ethical application, accountability, and commitment to the common good.

Leadership effectiveness, therefore, cannot be reduced to simplistic dichotomies—democracy versus autocracy, ethical versus corrupt governance, success versus failure. Instead, leadership must be assessed by its ability to uphold fundamental values such as service, responsibility, and care—three essential pillars that define its lasting impact on individuals, institutions, and society as a whole. As Northouse (2021) emphasizes, effective leadership integrates ethical decision-making with a commitment to justice and equity, ensuring that power serves collective rather than personal interests. These three pillars—the power of service, the power of responsibility, and the power of care—form the ethical foundation of true leadership. Leaders who embody these principles foster trust, inspire meaningful change, and build resilient institutions that sustain ethical governance and long-term effectiveness.

The Power of Service

True leadership is fundamentally an act of service, not a means of self-aggrandizement. Leaders entrusted with power—whether in public office, corporate governance, or civil society—must act as stewards of the common good rather than as rulers seeking personal gain. As Lao Tzu wisely stated, "To govern is to serve, not to rule" (Lao Tzu, 1972), reinforcing the principle that leadership exists for the benefit of those it serves rather than for the consolidation of personal authority. This perspective aligns with Greenleaf's (1977) Servant Leadership model, which emphasizes that "the servant-leader is servant first," prioritizing the needs of others above self-interest (p. 13).

Service-driven leadership ensures that policies and decisions advance collective well-being rather than benefit a privileged few. In government, leaders committed to public service work toward policies that protect human rights, promote social equity, and build resilient communities. Ethical governance is not merely about wielding authority but about creating conditions where justice and fairness prevail. John Rawls (1971), in *A Theory of Justice,* argued that a just society is one in which its most vulnerable members are not left behind. Leadership rooted in service aligns with this principle, fostering systems that prioritize equity and sustainability over short-term political or financial gains.

President Theodore Roosevelt powerfully expressed this idea by emphasizing that public leaders must be held accountable to the people they serve:

The President is merely the most important among a large number of public servants. He should be supported or opposed exactly to the degree which is warranted by his good conduct or bad conduct, his efficiency or inefficiency in rendering loyal, able, and disinterested service to the Nation as a whole. Therefore, it is absolutely necessary that there should be full liberty to tell the truth about his acts, and this means that it is exactly necessary to blame him when he does wrong as to praise him when he does right. Any other attitude in an American citizen is both base and servile. To announce that there must be no criticism of the President, or that we are to stand by the President, right or wrong, is not only unpatriotic and servile, but is morally treasonable to the American public. Nothing but the truth should be spoken about him or anyone else. But it is even more important to tell the truth, pleasant or unpleasant, about him than about anyone else. (Roosevelt, 1918, p. 149).

This statement underscores a key aspect of leadership: Service is not about blind loyalty or unquestioned authority—it requires accountability, transparency, and a commitment to the truth. Leaders in public service must not only embrace the responsibility of governance but also accept scrutiny as an essential component of ethical leadership.

In business, service-oriented leaders champion corporate responsibility by embedding ethics and sustainability into their decision-making processes. Paul Polman, the former CEO of Unilever, exemplified this approach by advancing stakeholder capitalism—aligning profit-making with long-term sustainability and social impact. Polman (2014) asserted, "Business must reconnect with society's needs," highlighting the imperative for companies to go beyond profit-maximization toward a broader social purpose. Economist Mariana Mazzucato (2018), in *The Value of Everything*, further argues that governments and businesses should not merely regulate markets but actively shape them to foster public welfare and long-term innovation.

Public service leadership is more about servicing than steering (Denhardt & Denhardt, 2000) and it extends beyond elected officials

(Bowman & West, 2021). Educators, healthcare professionals, and civil society leaders play vital roles in ensuring equitable access to knowledge, resources, and opportunities. Their work reflects the essence of service-driven leadership, emphasizing justice, accountability, and empowerment. Pope Francis (2015) reminds us that "service to the common good" (para. 129) is a fundamental responsibility of every individual and sector in society, calling on all to contribute to the flourishing of all through just relationships. He emphasizes that true leadership is rooted in service, highlighting the profound connection between serving others and fostering a more just and thriving society.

Moreover, the strength of public institutions is essential in counterbalancing corporate overreach, ensuring that democracy remains safeguarded against private interests. Effective leadership in public service requires not only ethical commitments but also the resilience to resist undue influence and uphold democratic values. By fostering institutions that serve rather than exploit, leadership rooted in service can build trust, social cohesion, and long-term progress. Ciulla (2004) argues, "Leadership is not just about moral intentions; it is about moral effectiveness" (p. 13), reinforcing the necessity for service-oriented leadership that translates values into action.

Ultimately, a system that values service over personal ambition ensures that governance—whether in politics, business, or civil society—remains an instrument for the common good rather than a tool for elite control. Prioritizing a leadership mindset centered on service and making decisions through the lens of stewardship can promote institutions that truly advance justice, equity, and sustainability for all.

The Power of Responsibility

Winston Churchill (1943) once said, "The price of greatness is responsibility"—a truth that sits at the heart of ethical leadership. Leadership without responsibility risks descending into unchecked power and moral decay. True leaders do not merely make decisions; they take ownership of their consequences. As Abraham Lincoln (1854) noted, "No man is good enough to govern another man without the other's consent"—a statement underscoring the ethical legitimacy rooted in accountability. This perspective aligns with Max Weber's view (1947) that legitimate authority stems not from coercion but from responsible accountability to the people. Similarly, Stephen Covey emphasized that "responsibility" means the ability to choose your response to situations, "Look at the word responsibility- 'response-ability'- the ability to choose your response. Highly proactive people recognize that responsibility. They do not blame circumstances, conditions, or conditioning for their behavior. Their behavior is a product of their own conscious choice, based on values, rather than a product of their conditions, based on a feeling" (Covey, 1997, p. 87).

Responsibility in leadership is marked by integrity, consistency, and a commitment to justice. Leaders like Jacinda Ardern, who navigated the COVID-19 crisis with empathy and transparency, and Mary Barra, who prioritized ethics during General Motors' crisis response, show how accountability fosters trust and resilience. As Warren Bennis (1989) asserted, "Leadership is the capacity to translate vision into reality through responsibility and integrity" (p. 39).

Madeleine Albright offers a powerful case study in responsible leadership. In *Fascism: A Warning* (2019) she writes, "Who has the responsibility to uphold human rights? The answer to that is: everyone." (p. 157). A refugee from Nazi-fascist Czechoslovakia, Albright understood the weight of responsible-moral leadership in sharp contrast to irresponsible-abusive leadership. As U.S. Ambassador to the UN, she played a pivotal role in shaping the American response to the 1995 Srebrenica massacre and her advocacy for humanitarian interventions helped establish the Responsibility to Protect (R2P) doctrine—an international commitment to prevent mass atrocities.

Leaders who evade responsibility often shift blame, manipulate narratives, or prioritize self-preservation over accountability. Political and corporate scandals—ranging from financial fraud to governance failures—are often traced back to leaders who refuse to acknowledge mistakes or take corrective action. Ronald Reagan's statement that "All of us together, in and out of government, must bear the burden" (Reagan, 1981) reminds us that leadership is a shared responsibility. Leaders must be willing to stand by their principles, make difficult ethical choices, and accept the weight of governance. Similarly, Dietrich Bonhoeffer (1949) argued that "Action springs not from thought, but from a readiness for responsibility," emphasizing that ethical leadership demands active engagement rather than passive reflection. Ultimately, ethical leadership requires more than rhetorical commitments—it demands accountability rooted in public service to others. Being accountable is not optional; it is the ethical duty of every leader committed to justice, integrity, and the common good.

The Power of Care

The most impactful leaders do not lead solely with strategy and vision—they lead with care, compassion, and empathy. Leadership is not about exerting control but about creating environments where people can thrive. As Theodore Roosevelt wisely stated, "People don't care how much you know until they know how much you care." Simon Sinek reinforces this principle, emphasizing that "Leadership is not about being in charge. It is about taking care of those in your charge" (Sinek, 2014, p. 7).

Genuine leadership is measured not by authority or power but by the well-being of those it serves. Mahatma Gandhi echoes this sentiment, stating, "The true measure of any society can be found in how it treats its most vulnerable members" (Gandhi, n.d.), reminding us that leadership carries a moral duty to protect and uplift those most at risk. Whether in politics or business, leadership rooted in care fosters trust, stability, and social cohesion. Policies that prioritize education, healthcare, and social welfare reflect a leadership model that values people over power—one that builds not just organizations and economies, but stronger, more just societies.

The consequences of leadership devoid of care are stark. Neglect, inequality, and systemic exploitation thrive under leadership that lacks a human-centered approach. Dietrich Bonhoeffer warned of this, stating, "The ultimate test of a moral society is the kind of world that it leaves to its children" (Bonhoeffer, n.d.). Leaders who disregard the long-term impact of their decisions jeopardize social and environmental sustainability, leading to instability and injustice, and possibly effective catastrophic consequences.

Hannah Arendt's study of Adolf Eichmann, a key organizer of the Holocaust, led her to conclude that the most dangerous leaders are not always fanatical or overtly cruel but rather careless individuals and thoughtless functionaries who follow orders without moral reflection. In *Eichmann in Jerusalem: A Report on the Banality of Evil* (1963), she observed that Eichmann was not driven by deep hatred but by blind obedience and bureaucratic efficiency, embodying a form of careless leadership that enabled mass atrocities. She warned that indifference and a failure to think critically about one's actions can lead to devastating consequences, as leaders who lack care distance themselves from the human cost of their decisions. This moral apathy is what allows authoritarian systems to thrive, turning ordinary individuals into agents of oppression. Leadership without care is not just negligent—it is a breeding ground for systemic injustice and destruction (Arendt, 1963/2006).

Benito Mussolini's fascist slogan *"Me ne frego"* ("I don't care") epitomizes the ruthless indifference that authoritarian regimes cultivate to justify oppression and violence. This phrase, popular among fascist *Camice Nere* (Blackshirt, paramilitary squads) glorified recklessness, blind obedience, and a disregard for human suffering, reinforcing a leadership mindset that valued power and domination over ethical responsibility (Gentile, 2005b).

In stark contrast, Don Lorenzo Milani, an inclusive, innovative educator and Catholic priest committed to social justice, countered this ideology with the opposite slogan: "I CARE." Milani's philosophy rejected the apathy and cruelty embedded in fascist rhetoric, instead promoting responsibility, solidarity, and moral consciousness. He famously declared, "I Care is the motto of those who cannot accept that things remain as they are" (Milani, 1967/2004), underscoring the power of education to cultivate engaged, and empathetic citizens. While fascism demanded submission and indifference, Milani's anti-fascist education empowered the marginalized to think critically, stand for justice, and actively shape a more equitable society (Tavanti & Wilp, 2021).

Unchecked authority fosters corruption and injustice. John Adams cautioned, "Because power corrupts, society's demands for moral authority and character increase as the importance of the position increases" (Adams, 1776). Without accountability, tyrants manipulate laws, silence dissent, and sacrifice the well-being of their people for personal gain. Plato further warns of the dangers of apathy, "The price of apathy towards public affairs is to be ruled by evil men" (Plato, 4th century BCE). When leaders do not care about the impact of their actions, they erode democracy, exploit the vulnerable, and create legacies of destruction—not just for the oppressed but ultimately for themselves.

Caring leadership is not passive—it is a proactive commitment to justice, inclusion, and social responsibility. President Dwight Eisenhower emphasized the moral implications of leadership decisions, stating, "Every gun that is made, every warship launched, every rocket fired signifies in the final sense, a theft from those who hunger and are not fed, those who are cold and are not clothed" (Eisenhower, 1953). True leadership requires shifting resources and priorities toward constructive, rather than destructive, ends, ensuring that power is exercised with wisdom, compassion, and a deep sense of responsibility for the greater good.

Leadership as People Power

In democratic societies, leadership ultimately belongs to the people. No matter how powerful, charismatic, or authoritative a leader may become, their mandate derives not from divine right or brute force but from the consent and vigilance of the governed. Leadership in a democracy is not a license to command unchecked but a privilege to serve, scrutinized continuously by the very people who elevate it. Even when those in power exhibit authoritarian tendencies—through suppression of dissent, manipulation of media, or the erosion of institutions—it remains the duty of the populace to resist such overreach (Bezio & Goethals, 2020). Democracy does not self-sustain; it relies on active participation, critical awareness, and, when necessary, courageous opposition. Civil resistance is not only a right; it is a responsibility when leadership veers from democratic norms and justice (Chenoweth, 2021).

At the same time, democratic citizenship also demands discernment. Not all resistance is virtuous, nor is all leadership suspect. The people also have the responsibility to support leaders during moments of moral courage, when difficult decisions must be made in service of justice, equity, and long-term collective good—even when those decisions are unpopular or costly in the short term. This nuanced relationship between leadership and the people—of scrutiny, resistance, and support—has been widely explored in political theory, civil society scholarship, and social movement studies.

Throughout my academic journey I've learned that resistance to leadership is not a binary choice but rather exists along a range of actions. It goes from symbolic gestures to institutional pushback, from peaceful protest to active defiance, and sometimes to revolutionary action (Tavanti, 2003).

Table 1.2 introduces various types of resistance to political leadership, outlining how and why opposition emerges in democratic societies. It describes the different forms and intensities of resistance that can arise when leaders either diverge from or align too closely with specific ideological, cultural, or policy values held by segments of the population. These responses can range from peaceful protests and civil disobedience to more organized political opposition, media criticism, and grassroots mobilization. The table also highlights how resistance is not solely reactive but can serve as a vital mechanism of accountability, helping to preserve democratic norms and ensure that leadership remains responsive to public needs and ethical standards. Understanding these dynamics is essential for analyzing the health and resilience of democratic systems.

Table 1.2: Resistance to Political Leadership

Type of Resistance (Intensity)	Description	Example Actions
Everyday Resistance (Low)	Subtle, often personal acts of resistance woven into ordinary life.	Deliberate inefficiency, non-cooperation, cultural resilience, passive defiance
Symbolic Expressive (Low)	Public signaling of agreement or dissent, often peaceful and performative.	Protests, public statements, artistic dissent, symbolic attire, online activism
Intellectual Ideological (Low–Moderate)	Thoughtful critique and reframing that upholds democratic discourse and accountability.	Public essays, alternative media, academic critique, civic education
Institutional (Moderate)	Working within established legal and political systems to challenge or support leadership.	Legislative opposition, legal suits, internal advocacy, whistleblowing
Economic (Moderate)	Leveraging financial tools to influence or resist political decisions.	Strikes, boycotts, divestment, refusal to pay for unjust systems
Civil Disobedience (Moderate–High)	Nonviolent but deliberate lawbreaking to expose injustice or demand reform.	Sit-ins, mass mobilization, refusal to comply with unjust policies

Underground / Covert (Moderate–High)	Hidden resistance aiming to subvert or destabilize leadership from within or below.	Leaks, encrypted communication, samizdat publishing, covert sabotage
Violent Resistance (High)	Direct and forceful opposition to illegitimate or oppressive authority.	Armed uprisings, riots, sabotage, revolutionary movements

Resistance to political leadership can only be truly understood in relation to power, which is not merely as something held by leaders but as something embedded in culture, norms, and everyday life. Antonio Gramsci, writing from prison under Mussolini's fascist regime, developed the concept of hegemony to explain how leadership is sustained not only through coercion but through consent. He observed that in hegemonic systems, the ruling class's worldview becomes so embedded in the cultural fabric that it appears as "common sense," rather than ideology.

As Gramsci states, "The supremacy of a social group manifests itself in two ways, as 'domination' and as 'intellectual and moral leadership'... A social group can, and indeed must, already exercise 'leadership' before winning governmental power" (Gramsci, 1971, p. 57). In fascist Italy, this meant shaping the cultural and ideological terrain—through media, religion, education, and public rituals—so that even the working class came to support a regime that ultimately worked against its own interests.

Gramsci emphasized that fascist hegemony was sustained through a kind of cultural education, "Every relationship of 'hegemony' is necessarily an educational relationship... it is also always a relationship of a pedagogical nature" (Gramsci, 1971, p. 350). Institutions like the Catholic Church, schools, newspapers, and popular culture were mobilized to normalize the fascist worldview. Importantly, Gramsci distinguished between a "war of maneuver" (direct political confrontation) and a "war of position" (a long-term cultural struggle to shift societal norms). For him, true resistance required not only challenging fascist institutions but also unlearning the fascist common sense—replacing it with new narratives and values. As he famously wrote, "To tell the truth, to arrive together at the truth, is a communist and revolutionary act" (Gramsci, as cited in Forgacs, 2000, p. 176).

Additionally, Michel Foucault argued that power is not centralized in institutions alone but flows through discourses, relationships, and everyday practices. Power, he noted, is not solely repressive but productive, "It produces things, it induces pleasures, forms of knowledge, produces discourse... a productive network that runs through the whole social body" (Foucault, 1982, p. 225).

For Foucault, wherever power is exercised, resistance is also possible. Resistance, therefore, should not only react to domination but also imagine alternatives—new ways of living, thinking, and relating. In this light, the responsibility of people in democratic societies is twofold: To resist hegemonic or authoritarian power when it threatens justice, and to support virtuous leadership when it upholds dignity and equality.

Resistance, like governance (as we will explore in Chapter 2), exists on a spectrum. And to counter the productive force of authoritarian power, resistance itself must become productive—generating new values, viable institutions, and inclusive futures (Bloom, 2016). The task is not only to resist what is, but to create what could be.

Leadership as Moral Intelligence

The call to create what could be naturally brings us to the question of leadership—not just as a position of authority, but as a moral and imaginative act. If resistance must be productive, then so too must leadership. What emerges from the analysis of power and resistance is a deeper understanding: That leadership is fundamentally a moral endeavor, not merely a mechanism of command or influence. It is defined less by ideological leanings—whether conservative or progressive, relational or task-oriented—and more by a leader's ability to navigate complexity with ethical clarity and emotional depth.

As Niccolò Machiavelli observed, "The first method for estimating the intelligence of a ruler is to look at the men he has around him" (Machiavelli, 1532). Leadership, therefore, cannot be reduced to strategy or charisma alone—it must be guided by a constellation of 'intelligences' such as: cognitive intelligence (IQ), emotional intelligence (EQ), cultural intelligence (CQ), social intelligence (SQ), and, crucially, moral intelligence (MQ). This multifaceted understanding of intelligence allows leaders to hold tension, navigate ambiguity, and exercise power responsibly in service of the common good (Gardner, 1983; Goleman, 1995; Lennick & Kiel, 2005).

A mentor of mine once offered me an insight when I was struggling to make sense of authoritarian leaders in international institutions. At the time, I assumed the authoritarian behavior was due merely to the leader's political views. But my mentor explained to me, "There are only two kinds of leaders—intelligent and inept." Upon first impression, the idea seemed too simple to be accurate. But over time, I have come to realize its significance. Intelligent leaders are those who allow experience—especially the suffering and dignity of others—to transform their worldview.

I witnessed this kind of transformation in leaders like Monsignor Óscar Romero of El Salvador and especially Bishop Samuel Ruiz García ("*Tatik*"—father) of Chiapas, with whom I had the privilege to work. Both men entered their pastoral roles with relatively conservative perspectives, shaped by institutional norms and traditional hierarchies. Yet, through direct encounters with the realities of poverty, violence, and systemic exclusion, their leadership evolved. They listened to the people, bore witness to their pain, and let that witness reshape their convictions. They became prophetic voices, not because they sought radicalism but because they were intelligent enough to be changed by truth on the ground (Perrin, 2015; Tavanti, 2003).

Their journeys also reveal a deeper truth. The most effective leaders are those who allow their experience to deepen their understanding and broaden their moral imagination. Transformation doesn't come from ideology alone but from the willingness to see, listen, and be changed. The most effective leaders are those who cultivate and integrate these diverse forms of intelligence, allowing them to read complex situations, adapt with discernment, and inspire trust across diverse communities. Leadership, then, is not merely about holding power—it is about exercising it with wisdom, integrity, and a deep commitment to justice, equity, and collective well-being. True leadership recognizes that influence is earned not through dominance, but through ethical vision and the capacity to serve something greater than oneself.

| 2 |

DECODING THE GOVERNANCE SPECTRUM

Many forms of government have been tried, and will be tried in this world of sin and woe. No one pretends that democracy is perfect or all-wise. Indeed, it has been said that democracy is the worst form of Government except for all those other forms that have been tried from time to time...

— **Winston Churchill, 1947**

Governance systems around the world do not fit neatly into singular categories. Instead, they exist on a spectrum, where different models frequently overlap, evolve, and blend with one another. Political scientists have long attempted to classify governance structures, yet no single framework fully encapsulates the complexity of how power is exercised across different societies. According to Linz (2000), contemporary political systems generally fall into three broad categories: democracies, totalitarian regimes, and authoritarian regimes, with hybrid systems occupying the space between them. Some scholars further distinguish monarchies as either distinct entities or hybrid structures within these main categories (Dahl, 2008; Fukuyama, 2014).

Additionally, dictatorship is often categorized as either a subset of authoritarianism or totalitarianism, highlighting the fluid and evolving nature of political systems (Levitsky & Way, 2020). These classifications serve as analytical tools, but in practice, many governments exhibit characteristics of multiple systems.

The complexity of governance is not new. Ancient political philosophy also sought to define different regime types. Plato, in *The Republic*, identified five types of government: aristocracy, timocracy, oligarchy, democracy, and tyranny (Plato, trans. 2004). While these classifications have evolved, the fundamental tensions between elite rule, popular sovereignty, and authoritarian control remain relevant. Modern political analysts caution against viewing governance in a binary framework, such as democracy versus dictatorship, since many regimes exist in hybrid forms (Diamond, 2019). This chapter moves beyond simplistic distinctions and instead focuses on six critical governance types that illustrate the spectrum of political authority in the modern world:

Liberal Democracy (Most Participatory): *Governance Through Inclusion and Debate* – A system that emphasizes pluralism, civil liberties, and robust democratic institutions (Dahl, 2006).

Technocratic Oligarchy: *Rule by Experts*—Promise and Peril – Governance dominated by technocrats, where expertise is valued over mass participation (Habermas, 2023).

Illiberal Democracy: *When Democracies Stop Being Democratic* – Democratically elected governments that erode civil liberties and undermine democratic norms (Zakaria, 2007).

Populist Authoritarianism: *Leadership Through Demagoguery* – A system where charismatic leaders use nationalist rhetoric and mass mobilization to consolidate power (Mounk, 2022; Mudde & Rovira Kaltwasser, 2017).

Oligarchic Autocracy: *Power Concentration and Wealth as Governance Tools* – A model where economic elites and political leaders form mutually reinforcing power structures (Winters, 2011).

Fascism (Most Authoritarian): *The Collapse of Democratic Institutions* – The most extreme form of authoritarianism, where centralized power, nationalism, and suppression of opposition define governance (Paxton, 2005).

By examining these governance types, this chapter aims to provide a nuanced understanding of how leadership functions within different political systems, highlighting their strengths, vulnerabilities, and long-term implications for societal stability. As Levitsky and Ziblatt (2018) argue, "democracies rarely collapse overnight; they erode gradually, often through legal and institutional manipulation rather than outright coups" (p. 5). Understanding these dynamics is essential for recognizing how governance models adapt to changing political, economic, and social forces.

Additional Governance Typologies

While the six governance types discussed in this chapter provide a broad framework for understanding modern political systems, additional forms of governance exist that capture unique historical and regional dynamics. Below is an expanded list of governance models that illustrate variations in power distribution, legitimacy, and political control across different societies. These governance forms are arranged in a roughly chronological order, from the oldest to the most recent. However, it is important to note that many of these older forms continue to exist in contemporary governance and leadership practices.

Theocracy: *Rule by Religious Authority* – One of the oldest governance systems, where religious institutions or leaders hold supreme authority. Examples include the rule of Egyptian pharaohs, medieval papal governance, and Iran's clerical rule (Arjomand, 2019).

Autocracy: *Centralized Personal Rule* – A system where supreme authority is vested in a single leader, whose decisions face little or no institutional constraint. Unlike oligarchic autocracy, which distributes power among elites, pure autocracy places governing power in the hands of one individual—be it a dictator, emperor, or authoritarian president. Examples include North Korea under Kim Jong-un and Belarus under Lukashenko (Linz, 2000).

Absolute Monarchy: *Unchecked Rule by a Sovereign* – A hereditary system where the monarch wields unrestricted power. Historically dominant in the Middle Ages and early modern period, as seen in France under Louis XIV and contemporary Saudi Arabia (Huntington, 2004).

Stratocracy: *Direct Military Governance* – A system where military leaders directly control the government, seen in ancient Sparta and modern Myanmar (Finer, 2017).

Plutocracy: *Governance by the Wealthy* – Plutocracy refers to a system in which a small minority of the wealthiest individuals rule or hold dominant influence. Historically, plutocratic tendencies were evident in ancient civilizations like Rome and Venice, where economic elites disproportionately influenced politics. Today, similar patterns can be seen in corporate lobbying and wealth-driven policymaking that curtail meaningful civic engagement and limited opportunities to live outside the values shaped by corporate and material interests (Winters, 2011).

Gerontocracy: *Rule by Elders* – A form of governance where leadership is concentrated among the elderly, historically common in tribal societies and seen in the Soviet Union under Brezhnev (Putnam, 1973).

Ethnocracy: *Rule by a Dominant Ethnic Group* – A system where political power is concentrated in the hands of a specific ethnic group, historically seen in colonial regimes, apartheid-era South Africa, and some contemporary nationalist states (Yiftachel, 2021).

Constitutional Monarchy: *Monarch as a Symbolic Figurehead* – Evolved as a response to absolute monarchy, where a monarch exists but real power is exercised by elected officials. Examples include the UK, Japan, and Sweden (Bogdanor, 1995).

Corporate State (Corporatism): *Governance by Economic and Social Interest Groups* – Developed during the industrial era, corporatist systems prioritize economic cooperation between business, labor, and the state. Seen in Fascist Italy under Mussolini and modern Singapore (Schmitter, 2020).

Military Junta: *Rule by the Armed Forces* – A modern form of military control where officials seize power and suspend civilian institutions. Seen in Argentina (1976–1983), Myanmar (post-2021), and Thailand (2014-2019) (Nordlinger, 2009).

Bureaucratic Authoritarianism: *Rule by Technocrats and State Institutions* – A 20th-century development where decision-making is dominated by unelected technocrats, found in post-coup Latin American regimes and China's centralized bureaucratic state (O'Donnell, 2019).

Anocracy: *A Fragile Mix of Autocracy and Democracy* – Emerging in post-colonial states, anocracies combine democratic and authoritarian elements but lack stability. Many African and Middle Eastern nations have experienced anocratic rule (Marshall & Gurr, 2020).

Hybrid Regime: *A Blend of Democratic and Authoritarian Features* – A contemporary model where electoral democracy exists but is undermined by state control over institutions. Russia, Turkey, and Hungary exemplify hybrid regimes (Levitsky & Way, 2020).

Kleptocracy: *Rule by Corruption* – A modern phenomenon where government leaders exploit public resources for personal gain. Examples include Mobutu Sese Seko's Zaire and post-Soviet oligarchic control in Russia (Collier, 2018).

Technocracy: *Rule of Experts* – A system of governance where decision-making is led by experts, scientists, and engineers rather than elected politicians. Technocracies prioritize data-driven policies, rational planning, and scientific management. Historical examples include the engineering-led economic policies of the Progressive Era in the United States and modern governance models in Singapore (Esmark, 2020).

Cyberocracy: *Governance by Digital and AI Systems* – Theoretical and emerging, cyberocracy refers to a system of governance increasingly influenced—or even dominated—by artificial intelligence, big data analytics, and algorithmic decision-making. Rather than relying solely on human judgment, power in a cyberocracy flows through networks of digital infrastructure, predictive models, and surveillance technologies. Some analysts identify China's digital surveillance state, with its integration of social credit systems and AI-powered monitoring, as a nascent form of cyberocracy (Brin, 1998). As these systems evolve, concerns have grown over the rise of **techno-fascism**—a form of authoritarian control that I explore in more detail in the last chapter. In this scenario, digital tools are not neutral instruments but mechanisms for centralized control, reducing transparency, eroding civil liberties, and replacing democratic deliberation with automated governance. The convergence of corporate data monopolies and state surveillance infrastructures further amplifies the potential for cyberocracy to evolve into an unaccountable and hyper-efficient mode of technocratic authoritarianism.

This expanded list acknowledges the vast complexity of governance models, emphasizing that political systems are neither fixed nor mutually exclusive. Many regimes incorporate elements from multiple governance types, adapting to shifting political, economic, and social conditions. A deep understanding of these diverse structures enhances our ability to critically analyze power dynamics, institutional resilience, and the evolving nature of leadership in the modern world.

While the governance types discussed so far provide a broad framework for analyzing political systems, there are numerous additional models that further illustrate the diversity of governance structures. Systems such as **aristocracy** (rule by the elite), **oligarchy** (rule by a small, powerful group), and **meritocracy** (rule based on ability and achievement) have historically influenced political leadership (Derbyshire & Derbyshire, 2016). Other governance forms like tribalism and feudalism were dominant in pre-modern societies and continue to shape governance in certain regions today. Meanwhile, **capitalism**, **socialism**, and **statism** emphasize economic structures as integral to governance.

Additionally, hybrid systems such as **corporatocracy** (domination by corporate interests), **electocracy** (rule by elected representatives with limited democratic participation), and **logocracy** (rule through ideology and discourse) highlight the complexity of modern political systems (Kurtz, 2020). More extreme forms, including **totalitarianism** (absolute centralized control), **military dictatorship** (authoritarian rule by military leaders), and **kakistocracy** (government by the least qualified or most corrupt), further demonstrate the breadth of governance models (Heywood, 2021). Some forms, such as **ecclesiocracy** (religious governance), **ergatocracy** (rule by workers), and **geniocracy** (rule by intellectuals), remain more theoretical or rare but continue to shape political thought.

Anarchy, often misconceived merely as the absence of governance, traditionally refers to decentralized, non-hierarchical systems rooted in voluntary cooperation (Graeber, 2013). Classical anarchists such as Proudhon, Bakunin, and Kropotkin envisioned self-managed societies built on mutual aid and collective decision-making (Marshall, 2009). However, the concept can also be understood as a form of *chaos-governance*, wherein those in power deliberately foster disorder or fragmentation—through strategies like *divide et impera*—to maintain centralized control and suppress collective agency (Cerise, 2023). In this light, anarchy is not always a lack of governance but can reflect a manipulative form of it, revealing how power operates through both visible institutions and invisible fractures. Understanding this spectrum is essential to evaluating leadership within diverse historical and contemporary frameworks.

Comparing the Governance Spectrum

Governance systems shape leadership styles and influence how citizens or followers engage with political structures. Each system fosters distinct leadership expectations, ranging from participatory and deliberative approaches to centralized and authoritarian models. Similarly, followers within these systems develop unique predispositions toward authority, decision-making, and civic engagement. Some governance models encourage active political participation and institutional trust, while others promote passivity, loyalty to a leader, or skepticism toward democratic norms. This section examines a spectrum of governance models, beginning with Liberal Democracy, the most participatory form, and progressing toward increasingly centralized and authoritarian structures. Understanding these variations provides insight into how different political environments cultivate distinct leadership behaviors and citizen responses.

1. Liberal Democracy (Most Participatory)

Liberal democracy is characterized by deliberative, pluralistic, and consensus-building leadership, where governance is rooted in free elections, the rule of law, strong civil liberties, and institutional checks and balances (Dahl, 2006). Leaders in such systems emphasize dialogue, compromise, and institutional legitimacy to balance competing interests. Followers in liberal democracies tend to have a high tolerance for diversity, ideological pluralism, and complex decision-making processes. They value press freedom, institutional accountability, and civic engagement as essential to governance (Diamond, 2019). Citizens in these societies trust democratic institutions and international cooperation, believing in activism as a means of shaping public policy. Examples include Germany under Angela Merkel, Canada under Justin Trudeau, and New Zealand under Jacinda Ardern, as well as the United States in the pre-2016 era.

2. Technocratic Oligarchy

Technocratic oligarchy prioritizes expert-driven, managerial governance, where decision-making is based on meritocracy, data, and technological efficiency rather than mass political participation (Fischer, 1990; Habermas, 1992). This system often results in limited direct democracy, with power concentrated in the hands of specialists, corporate leaders, and institutional experts. Followers of technocratic governance place a premium on efficiency, expertise, and market-driven policies over ideological representation. They tend to trust technology, business leaders, and centralized institutions, supporting pragmatic and evidence-based solutions (Schmitter, 2020). This form of governance is demonstrated by Singapore under Lee Kuan Yew, the European Central Bank's decision-making model, and Silicon Valley-inspired governance frameworks such as Elon Musk's AI-driven governance theories.

3. Illiberal Democracy

Illiberal democracies retain competitive elections but undermine democratic institutions through weak judicial independence, press restrictions, and the expansion of executive power (Zakaria, 2021). Leaders in these regimes adopt a majoritarian and nationalist approach, where the electoral process legitimizes centralized control. Followers of illiberal democracies often distrust traditional democratic institutions, favoring majority rule with fewer constraints on government power (Levitsky & Way, 2020). They support nationalist policies that emphasize cultural identity while endorsing restrictions on opposition voices and media freedom. Such governance can be observed in Hungary under Viktor Orbán, Turkey under Recep Tayyip Erdoğan, India under Narendra Modi, and Russia during Vladimir Putin's early years.

4. Populist Authoritarianism

Populist authoritarian regimes rely on charismatic, emotionally driven leadership, where elected figures exploit nationalist sentiments, cultural grievances, and personalistic rule (Mounk, 2022; Mudde & Rovira Kaltwasser, 2017). These leaders position themselves as defenders of the "common people" against elites and external threats, often dismantling institutional constraints in the process. Followers in such systems seek strong leaders who promise to restore order and national identity. They are skeptical of mainstream media, elites, and global institutions, preferring emotionally charged rhetoric and loyalty over institutional legalism (Levitsky & Ziblatt, 2018). Populist authoritarianism has been evident in the governance styles of Donald Trump (especially in his efforts to erode democratic norms), Jair Bolsonaro in Brazil, and Rodrigo Duterte in the Philippines.

5. Oligarchic Autocracy

Oligarchic autocracies are elite-controlled regimes where power is consolidated within a small ruling class, often composed of political and corporate elites. Elections may exist but are manipulated to maintain control, while dissent is covertly repressed (Winters, 2011). Leadership in these systems is power-consolidating and repressive while maintaining a facade of legitimacy. Followers of oligarchic autocracies accept elite dominance in exchange for stability and economic security, often expressing skepticism about mass democracy. They tend to trust economic elites and corporate governance more than traditional political institutions, prioritizing financial prosperity over civic engagement (Derbyshire & Derbyshire, 2016). Contemporary examples include Vladimir Putin's Russia, where a small elite controls political and economic power, and Gulf monarchies such as the UAE and Saudi Arabia.

6. Fascism (Most Authoritarian)

Fascism represents the most extreme form of authoritarianism, where governance is ultra-nationalist, militarized, and totalitarian (Paxton, 2005). Fascist regimes operate under one-party rule, suppress opposition, and exert complete state control over society, often enforcing racial or ethnic hierarchies. Leaders in fascist systems emphasize national purity, militarization, and absolute loyalty to the state. Followers tend to exhibit extreme nationalism, rejecting pluralism and democratic values while supporting violent suppression of opposition and state-controlled propaganda (Heywood, 2021). Historically, fascist regimes have included the Nazi Party in Germany under Adolf Hitler (the National Socialist German Workers' Party), the Fascist Party in Italy under Benito Mussolini (Italian Socialist Republic), and Falangism in Spain under Francisco Franco (Falenge Español Tradicionalista). In addition, there were multiple regimes influenced by fascism such as the National Christian Party under Ion Antonescu in the Kingdom of Romania, the Ustaše in Croatia under Ante Pavelić, and the Arrow Cross Party in Hungary under Ferenc Szálasi (Blamires & Jackson 2006).

Dynamics Across Governance Models

Governance systems shape not only leadership styles but also the expectations and behaviors of its followers. Different political structures cultivate varying levels of participation, trust in institutions, and tolerance for opposition. While liberal democracies emphasize deliberation and institutional accountability, technocratic oligarchies prioritize efficiency and expert decision-making. Illiberal democracies and populist authoritarian regimes leverage majoritarian rule and strong leadership, often undermining institutional checks. More extreme forms, such as oligarchic autocracies and fascist regimes, consolidate power by restricting dissent and controlling public discourse.

Table 2.1 outlines the leadership styles, follower mindsets, and institutional dynamics across these governance types. It illustrates the stark differences in governance types, particularly in leadership styles and public engagement, and these dynamics remain highly relevant in contemporary political landscapes.

Table 2.1: Governance Typologies and Dynamics

GOVERNANCE TYPE	LEADERSHIP STYLE & FOLLOWER MINDSET	VIEW ON INSTITUTIONS, MEDIA & OPPOSITION
LIBERAL DEMOCRACY	Deliberative, participatory leadership; values pluralism, rational debate, activism	Trusts courts, press, global cooperation; media independent; opposition protected
TECHNOCRATIC OLIGARCHY	Expert-driven, managerial leadership; prefers efficiency, AI-driven decision-making	Trusts elite governance and markets; media limited to expert discourse; opposition irrelevant
ILLIBERAL DEMOCRACY	Majoritarian, nationalist leadership; supports majority rule, skeptical of globalism	Selectively trusts national institutions; media restricted; opposition suppressed if disruptive
POPULIST AUTHORITARIANISM	Charismatic, emotional leadership; seeks strong leader, distrusts elites	Distrusts liberal institutions; delegitimizes media; harasses the opposition

OLIGARCHIC AUTOCRACY	Elite-controlled, manipulative leadership; accepts elite control for stability	Only elite-controlled institutions matter; media controlled; opposition silenced
FASCISM	Ultra-nationalist, militarized leadership; seeks total control, purity, order	Destroys democratic institutions; media pure propaganda; opposition eliminated

Liberal democracies, such as Germany under Angela Merkel and Canada under Justin Trudeau, emphasize pluralism, institutional trust, and active civic participation, where independent media and judicial systems serve as essential checks on power (Dahl, 2006). In such societies, followers tend to value democratic institutions, press freedom, and global cooperation. However, the rise of misinformation and political polarization has challenged these ideals, with declining trust in traditional institutions even within democratic societies (Norris & Inglehart, 2019).

In contrast, technocratic oligarchies, such as Singapore under Lee Kuan Yew and elements of European Union governance, prioritize expert-driven decision-making and efficiency over mass political participation (McDonnell & Valbruzzi, 2014). Today, this model is increasingly reflected in governance trends that emphasize AI-driven policymaking, corporate-led solutions, and managerial approaches to governance, such as Elon Musk's advocacy for data-driven and automation-focused administration. Followers of these systems often prefer expertise and stability over ideological debates, aligning with growing public trust in technology companies over traditional political structures (Gilbert & Mohseni, 2011).

As governance shifts toward illiberal democracy, leaders such as Viktor Orbán in Hungary and Narendra Modi in India have leveraged majoritarian rule, nationalist rhetoric, and institutional weakening to consolidate power while maintaining electoral legitimacy (Levitsky & Way, 2020). Followers of these systems tend to prioritize cultural identity and national sovereignty over liberal democratic norms, often supporting restrictions on media and opposition voices. Similarly, in populist authoritarian regimes, such as those led by Donald Trump and Jair Bolsonaro, leaders use charisma, anti-elitist rhetoric, and emotional appeals to cultivate loyal followers (Mudde & Rovira Kaltwasser, 2017). These movements thrive on distrust of mainstream institutions, fueling polarized political environments where followers embrace alternative media narratives and conspiracy theories over traditional sources of information (Norris & Inglehart, 2019).

At the most authoritarian end, oligarchic autocracies and fascist regimes consolidate power by silencing dissent, controlling media, and restricting public freedoms. In contemporary Russia, Vladimir Putin's governance exemplifies oligarchic autocracy, where a small elite dominates both economic and political systems, suppressing opposition and leveraging state-controlled propaganda (Eatwell, 2017). In China, Xi Jinping's leadership aligns more closely with authoritarian technocracy, where state surveillance, AI-driven governance, and strict ideological control define citizen engagement. The role of followers in such regimes is shaped by state narratives that promote stability, economic growth, and nationalistic loyalty over political freedoms.

These governance models illustrate how leadership strategies and follower mindsets evolve in response to societal needs and external challenges. The increasing influence of technology, the rise of misinformation, and the global polarization of political ideologies continue to shape governance in the 21st century, making it essential to understand these patterns in historical and contemporary contexts.

Leadership Across Government Types

Governance structures do not emerge in isolation; they are the result of complex interactions between leadership styles, the predispositions of followers, and the contextual forces that legitimize and sustain them. Just as ecological systems depend on interdependent relationships between organisms and environmental conditions, political systems function through dynamic interactions among leaders, institutions, and the social and economic forces shaping collective behavior. Different governance types arise and persist when specific leadership styles align with follower tendencies and external conditions that reinforce their authority. This section explores how these ecosystemic dynamics operate across six forms of governance.

In liberal democracies, governance is sustained by a participatory political culture, institutional safeguards, and an electorate that values deliberation and pluralism. Leaders in these systems often exhibit transformational, servant, and collaborative leadership, inspiring civic engagement, prioritizing public well-being, and navigating compromise within complex institutions. However, leadership alone does not sustain liberal democracy; its viability depends on a citizenry predisposed toward active participation, critical thinking, and institutional trust. Historical moments of crisis—such as economic downturns, wars, or civil rights movements—often serve as catalysts for reinforcing or challenging democratic ideals. For instance, the civil rights movement in the United States created conditions for transformational leadership, embodied by figures like Martin Luther King Jr., to push democratic institutions toward greater inclusivity. Conversely, declining trust in institutions, economic inequality, and political polarization can shift democracies toward illiberal tendencies, as seen in recent political disruptions across Europe and North America (Dahl, 2006).

Technocratic oligarchies emerge when expertise is privileged over mass participation, creating governance structures where decision-making is concentrated among specialists and elites. Leaders in these systems often exhibit bureaucratic, strategic, and technocratic leadership, emphasizing efficiency, long-term planning, and data-driven policymaking. However, these structures remain viable only when the public perceives them as legitimate—either due to economic prosperity, policy success, or the relative failure of more participatory governance models. Followers in technocratic systems tend to defer to expertise, trusting in rational decision-making rather than populist appeal. However, legitimacy can erode if technocratic elites become too insulated, leading to public discontent and the rise of more populist alternatives. The European Union's governance model, often criticized for its bureaucratic detachment, illustrates this tension, as does Singapore's highly efficient but politically constrained system under Lee Kuan Yew (Habermas, 2023).

Illiberal democracies emerge when elected governments erode democratic norms and institutions while retaining a façade of electoral legitimacy. This governance model relies on leaders who blend populist, authoritarian, and pragmatic styles, often employing nationalist rhetoric, media manipulation, and legal strategies to concentrate power. Yet, such systems are not sustained by leaders alone; they depend on a supportive base predisposed to favor stronger individual and national security, identity-driven politics, and a deep skepticism of pluralism. External shocks—such as migration crises, economic downturns, or perceived cultural threats—frequently create fertile ground for these illiberal tendencies to take hold and flourish. Viktor Orbán's Hungary exemplifies this ecosystem, where the leadership's nationalist agenda aligns with public anxieties about globalization and demographic change. These regimes persist when institutions fail to counterbalance executive overreach and when followers remain mobilized by a narrative of external threats and internal enemies (Zakaria, 2021).

Populist authoritarianism thrives in environments where democratic institutions are fragile, economic disparities are pronounced, and political elites are viewed as corrupt or ineffective. Leaders in these regimes often exhibit charismatic, strongman, and demagogic leadership, directly engaging with followers through emotional appeals and nationalistic messaging. However, such leadership alone is insufficient—populist authoritarianism requires a public predisposed toward distrust of elites and a desire for direct, decisive action. Crises, real or manufactured, play a crucial role in legitimizing these leaders, allowing them to position themselves as the sole solution to systemic problems. Donald Trump's rise in the United States and Jair Bolsonaro's leadership in Brazil were both facilitated by economic grievances, cultural polarization, and a widespread belief in institutional dysfunction. These leaders sustain power by maintaining high levels of emotional engagement with their base, often through media spectacle and confrontational rhetoric (Mounk, 2022; Mudde & Rovira Kaltwasser, 2017).

Oligarchic autocracies depend on a mutually reinforcing relationship between economic elites and political leaders, where wealth concentration translates into political control. Leaders in these systems often exhibit transactional, strategic, and authoritarian leadership, using patronage networks to maintain loyalty among key power holders. However, oligarchic autocracies are not sustained solely by leadership—they require a followership culture that accepts wealth as a legitimate basis for governance. In societies where economic mobility is low and political alternatives are constrained, people may come to see elite rule as inevitable or even beneficial. External factors such as resource wealth (e.g., oil rents in Saudi Arabia and Russia) or geopolitical conditions (e.g., Cold War alliances that supported autocratic regimes) further reinforce these systems. Vladimir Putin's Russia exemplifies this model, where political loyalty is exchanged for economic privileges, and dissent is systematically marginalized (Winters, 2011).

At the most extreme end of authoritarianism, fascist regimes emerge when democratic institutions collapse entirely, and governance is based on totalitarian control, mass mobilization, and ideological fanaticism. Leaders in these systems exhibit totalitarian, militaristic, and charismatic-dictatorial leadership, maintaining power through propaganda, coercion, and a cult of personality. However, like the leader–follower dynamics observed in illiberal democracies, fascism is not merely the outcome of dictatorial ambition; it also depends on a populace predisposed to authoritarian submission. Such predispositions are often shaped by prolonged social instability, economic collapse, or the collective memory of national humiliation—conditions that foster a yearning for order, unity, strong leadership, and cultural tolerance for power distance (Tavanti, 2012). The rise of Adolf Hitler in Germany was made possible not only by his own leadership but also by the widespread disillusionment following World War I, economic devastation during the Great Depression, and the failure of democratic institutions to restore stability. Fascist regimes also rely on bureaucratic enablers and military institutions willing to subordinate themselves to a totalitarian leader. Once established, they sustain themselves through fear, indoctrination, and the elimination of political opposition (Paxton, 2005).

Ecosystemic Lenses on Governance

Governance systems are dynamic and multifaceted, rarely fitting neatly into a single category. They operate more like evolving ecosystems, where various leadership styles interact with the values, expectations, and behaviors of followers, as well as with shifting contextual factors—such as economic pressures, cultural norms, and technological developments. These interactions can either reinforce political stability or create disruption and transformation, highlighting the complex, adaptive nature of governance in practice.

Liberal democracies depend on participatory and consensus-driven leadership, sustained by engaged citizens and resilient institutions. Technocratic oligarchies thrive when expertise is valued, and economic stability legitimizes non-participatory governance. Illiberal democracies and populist authoritarian regimes emerge when economic or cultural crises create demand for strong, nationalist leadership that weakens democratic norms. Oligarchic autocracies persist when wealth and power remain concentrated, and alternatives are suppressed. Fascist regimes, the most extreme form of authoritarianism, arise in conditions of institutional collapse and existential crisis, where totalitarian leadership finds mass support.

Understanding governance through an ecosystemic lens highlights the dynamic interplay between leadership, followership, and context. Leadership styles alone do not determine governance outcomes—public predispositions, institutional strength, and external crises all shape the conditions under which certain governance models rise and fall. This perspective is essential for assessing political stability, anticipating shifts in power, and developing strategies for sustaining democratic governance in an era of increasing political volatility.

Yet, while the governance spectrum captures a wide array of systems, it is not a fixed continuum; governance is in constant flux, shaped by pressures both internal and external. Transformations in governance occur when power structures, political norms, and institutional frameworks shift, sometimes gradually and sometimes through abrupt ruptures. The erosion of democratic norms, the consolidation of autocratic control, or even the reinvigoration of participatory governance can be seen as part of a broader evolutionary process—one influenced by societal demands, technological disruptions, and geopolitical realignments.

To understand how governance evolves, it is necessary to move beyond static classifications and examine the transformative processes that reshape political landscapes. How do democracies backslide into authoritarianism? Under what conditions do authoritarian regimes liberalize? What role do social movements, economic shocks, and global governance trends play in these transitions?

In the following chapter, we delve into these questions, exploring the mechanisms through which governance models adapt, break down, or reinvent themselves. By examining historical case studies, contemporary shifts, and theoretical frameworks, we aim to decode the forces that drive governance transformations in an increasingly complex and uncertain world.

| 3 |

DECODING GOVERNANCE TRANSFORMATIONS

> *Men make their own history, but they do not make it as they please; they do not make it under self-selected circumstances, but under circumstances existing already, given and transmitted from the past.*
>
> **— Karl Marx, 1852**

Leadership theories have long attempted to decode the role of leaders in shaping organizations and societies. Early perspectives, such as the Great Man theory, framed leadership as the domain of exceptional individuals—charismatic visionaries or powerful rulers who single-handedly directed the course of history (Carlyle, 1841; Bass, 1990). This perspective dominated leadership thought for much of the 19th and early 20th centuries, reinforcing the idea that leaders are born, not made. As research evolved, theories like Situational Leadership (Hersey & Blanchard, 1969) and Contingency theory (Fiedler, 1967) challenged this notion, arguing that leadership effectiveness depends on the interaction between leaders and their circumstances. These models highlight that leadership is not solely about individual traits but also about how leaders respond to challenges, crises, and opportunities within their specific environments.

However, leadership is not a one-directional force. While leaders influence change, they are also shaped by the broader social, economic, and political forces at play. The *Zeitgeist* (spirit of the times) theory of leadership (Murthy & McKie, 2008; Tolstoy, 1869; Spencer, 1896) challenges the notion of individual dominance in historical progress, arguing that the spirit of the times—collective movements, institutional structures, and societal shifts—creates the conditions that elevate certain leaders. This theory suggests that leadership does not emerge in a vacuum but instead reflects societal needs and systemic readiness for transformation. A transformational leader may rise not simply because of personal attributes but because a society or organization is primed for change, creating an opportunity for certain leadership styles to thrive (Burns, 1978). This idea aligns with more recent research in adaptive leadership (Heifetz, 1994), which emphasizes that effective leadership is deeply contextual and emerges in response to evolving societal demands.

This dynamic interaction between leadership and systemic evolution is particularly critical when examining the evolution of governance. Political systems shift in response to economic transformations, wars, technological advancements, and ideological currents—changes that both empower and constrain leaders (North, 1990; Fukuyama, 2011). Democratic transitions, authoritarian backsliding, and institutional reforms are often seen as outcomes of leadership decisions, yet they are equally shaped by structural conditions that define what kind of leadership is possible (Acemoglu & Robinson, 2012). To fully understand governance evolution, we must move beyond a leader-centric or system-centric view and instead examine the reciprocal relationship between leaders and the broader forces that shape them. By doing so, we can better analyze how leaders navigate, exploit, or challenge systemic changes, and in turn, how political and institutional shifts create or dismantle opportunities for different types of leadership.

How Governance Evolves and Leaders Emerge

Governance is not static; it evolves in response to economic, social, technological, and political pressures, shaping the conditions in which leaders emerge and operate. Throughout history, governments have transitioned between different systems—monarchies to republics, authoritarian regimes to democracies, and centralized states to decentralized networks—depending on societal needs and external disruptions. While leadership theories often focus on how individuals shape political structures, an equally important question is how political systems shape the leaders who rise to prominence. The interplay between governance evolution and leadership emergence is crucial to understanding historical transformations and contemporary political trends.

The evolution of governance follows structural and cyclical patterns, influenced by both internal and external forces. Internally, political institutions either strengthen or weaken based on legitimacy, economic stability, and administrative efficiency. For instance, the collapse of the Roman Republic into an imperial dictatorship under Augustus was not solely due to his leadership but was enabled by a crisis of governance—widespread corruption, elite factionalism, and economic disparity (Syme, 1939). Similarly, the transition from feudalism to modern nation-states in Europe occurred due to economic shifts such as the rise of mercantilism and early capitalism, which empowered monarchs to centralize authority at the expense of feudal lords (Tilly, 1992). Externally, governance evolves through wars, globalization, and ideological diffusion. The spread of democratic governance in the late 20th century, for example, was significantly influenced by international norms and economic liberalization following the Cold War (Huntington, 1991).

Just as governance adapts to structural transformations, leaders emerge in response to these systemic shifts. The Great Man theory suggests that exceptional individuals drive leadership, yet historical patterns suggest that leaders often emerge because of the political and social climate rather than despite it (Carlyle, 1841). The emergence of Franklin D. Roosevelt during the Great Depression, for example, was a direct consequence of economic collapse and societal demand for bold, interventionist leadership. Likewise, Napoleon Bonaparte rose to power amid the chaos of post-revolutionary France, capitalizing on a disorganized government and a public yearning for stability (Roberts, 2014). In contrast, some leaders fail to gain traction because the political environment is not conducive to their style of leadership. Reformist figures like Mikhail Gorbachev, who sought to liberalize the Soviet Union, faced significant institutional resistance and economic decline that ultimately led to the collapse of the USSR rather than a controlled transition to democracy (Brown, 1996).

This dynamic interaction between governance evolution and leadership emergence can be seen in the Contingency theory of leadership (Fiedler, 1967), which argues that no single leadership style is universally effective leaders must align with the conditions of their time. Authoritarian figures like Julius Caesar, Adolf Hitler, and Vladimir Putin emerged in moments of institutional weakness, social unrest, and economic uncertainty, leveraging crises to justify consolidating power. Conversely, democratic leaders like Nelson Mandela and Angela Merkel thrived in contexts where governance systems were robust enough to support deliberation, negotiation, and coalition-building (Bass, 1990). These examples demonstrate that leaders do not shape history in isolation—they are shaped by the systemic conditions in which they operate.

At the same time, the evolution of governance also depends on how leaders navigate and respond to systemic pressures. Some leaders accelerate institutional change—for instance, Theodore Roosevelt's Progressive Era policies redefined the role of government in regulating corporations, shaping modern governance in the U.S. (Dalton, 2012). Others resist change, attempting to preserve existing power structures even as societal pressures push for transformation, as seen in the authoritarian backsliding of Hungary under Viktor Orbán and Turkey under Recep Tayyip Erdoğan (Levitsky & Ziblatt, 2018). In many cases, leadership transitions signal broader shifts in governance—the rise of technocratic leaders in the 21st century reflects an increasing reliance on expertise and policy-driven decision-making over traditional populism (Fukuyama, 2011).

As governance evolves through economic shifts, wars, technological advancements, and ideological transformations, leaders emerge in ways that either accelerate, resist, or adapt to these changes. Some leaders act as an impetus for political transformation, leveraging crises and societal demands to implement sweeping reforms or revolutionary change. Others serve as barriers to progress, upholding entrenched power structures and resisting reform, often delaying inevitable transitions. Still, some leaders are products of their time, shaped more by historical forces than by personal ambition, responding to challenges rather than driving radical change.

Governance and leadership exist in a reciprocal relationship—governments evolve based on systemic pressures, and leaders emerge in response to these shifts, reinforcing or reshaping the trajectory of governance. By understanding this interplay, we can better analyze political transitions, predict leadership trends, and assess the long-term stability of different governing systems. Future governance models—whether AI-driven bureaucracies, decentralized political structures, or hybrid democracies—will continue to shape the kind of leaders who rise to prominence, just as those leaders will, in turn, redefine governance for future generations.

The following Table 3.1 categorizes key historical figures based on their roles in the evolution of governance, illustrating how individual leaders have influenced political systems—and how, in turn, their leadership has been shaped by broader systemic, social, and historical forces. From autocrats to reformers, these figures reflect the complex interplay between personal agency and institutional structures. Understanding governance evolution requires more than tracing formal changes in constitutions or regimes; it also involves examining how grassroots movements, ideological shifts, and popular demands contribute to shaping government transitions and redefining leadership legitimacy. By analyzing both top-down and bottom-up forces, we gain a fuller picture of how power is negotiated, contested, and transformed over time.

Table 3.1: Governance and Leadership Factors

Factor	How Governance Evolves	How Leaders Emerge
Economic Transformation	Transition from feudal economies to capitalist states led to the rise of nation-states.	Leaders like FDR during the Great Depression capitalized on economic crises to implement reforms.
Wars and Conflicts	Major wars often lead to changes in government structure, such as the fall of empires.	Napoleon rose during the French Revolutionary Wars, leveraging instability to consolidate power.
Social Movements and Civil Rights	Public pressure forces governments to expand rights, reform laws, and democratize.	Nelson Mandela emerged due to anti-apartheid struggles, shaping South Africa's democracy.
Technological Advancements	Technologies like the printing press and the internet reshaped governance and information control.	Tech-savvy leaders like Estonia's e-government pioneers emerged due to digital transformation.
Ideological Shifts	New political ideologies (liberalism, socialism, nationalism) influence governmental structures.	Vladimir Lenin used Marxist ideology to justify the Bolshevik Revolution and USSR governance.

INSTITUTIONAL STRENGTH OR WEAKNESS	Weak institutions enable authoritarian takeovers, while strong institutions ensure democratic resilience.	Hitler exploited the Weimar Republic's institutional failures to rise to power in Nazi Germany.
GLOBALIZATION AND INTERNATIONAL INFLUENCE	Exposure to international norms and global organizations pushes states toward governance changes.	Technocratic leaders, such as those in the EU, gained prominence through global economic policies.

Throughout history, grassroots mobilizations have challenged existing power structures, prompting transitions from monarchies to democracies, from authoritarianism to participatory governance, and from oligarchic rule to more inclusive systems. Movements advocating for civil rights, environmental justice, and economic equity have not only pressured governments to reform but have also produced leaders who gain legitimacy through public support rather than traditional institutional pathways. In an era of digital activism and decentralized advocacy, social movements continue to redefine leadership by amplifying marginalized voices, holding governments accountable, and shaping new governance paradigms. Therefore, to fully understand how governance evolves, we must analyze how social movements interact with institutions, influence policy, and legitimize new forms of leadership in response to societal demands.

Discontent Movements and Change Leaders

The rise of authoritarian, populist, and fascist leaders does not occur in isolation; it is often fueled by the energy and mobilization of social movements that create the conditions for their emergence. In Italy, movements like *Prima gli Italiani* ("Italians First")—championed by Matteo Salvini's Lega Nord and later amplified by Giorgia Meloni's Fratelli d'Italia—have fueled a surge in right-wing populism by appealing to national pride, resisting perceived bureaucratic impositions from the European Union, and stoking fears around immigration across the Mediterranean. These movements typically build their platforms around what Rodríguez-Pose (2020) describes as populism's "holy trinity": a discourse that pits the 'pure' people against a 'corrupt' elite, promotes anti-immigration sentiments as a defense of national identity, and mobilizes nationalism against foreign influences and supranational institutions like the EU.

Similarly, movements like Make America Great Again (MAGA) in the United States, Brexit in the United Kingdom, Bolsonarismo in Brazil, and the National Rally in France have provided platforms for leaders who challenge democratic norms while promoting nationalist, exclusionary, and often reactionary ideologies. These movements are not simply expressions of individual support for a leader but reflect broader shifts in public sentiment—whether frustration with globalization, fear of demographic changes, or disillusionment with political elites. The ability of authoritarian-leaning figures to rise to power is deeply connected to their capacity to harness these movements, frame themselves as their champions, and institutionalize their influence through state control and media dominance.

At the same time, social movements have also historically played crucial roles in positive social change, demonstrating that large-scale mobilization can also lead to greater justice, inclusion, and democracy rather than authoritarianism. The Civil Rights Movement in the United States, for example, was powerfully led by figures like Martin Luther King Jr., who used nonviolent resistance and powerful oratory to mobilize support and challenge segregation and discrimination. Similarly, the Women's Suffrage Movement, which spanned multiple countries, fought for women's right to vote, with leaders like Susan B. Anthony in the United States and Emmeline Pankhurst in the United Kingdom playing crucial roles in advocating for and organizing around this cause. The Anti-Apartheid Movement in South Africa, led by Nelson Mandela, successfully dismantled racial segregation, showing how long-term activism can result in radical but positive systemic change. The Abolitionist Movement, which aimed to end slavery, saw leaders like Frederick Douglass and William Lloyd Garrison use their platforms to expose the evils of slavery and advocate for its abolition. Labor movements around the world, including the rise of trade unions, successfully fought for workers' rights, fair wages, and humane working conditions. More recently, the LGBTQ+ Rights Movement has led to significant progress in securing legal protections and social acceptance for LGBTQ+ individuals. With figures like Harvey Milk, the first openly gay man elected to public office in California, playing a pivotal role in advancing equality. Environmental movements, such as those led by Jane Goodall and Greta Thunberg, have shifted global conversations toward sustainability and the urgent need for climate action. These examples highlight how movements, when guided by democratic principles and inclusive leadership, can push societies toward progress rather than regression.

Table 3.2 shows how discontent movements have fueled authoritarian and populist leaders in times of crisis. From Hitler's exploitation of Germany's economic collapse to Stalin's consolidation of power after the Bolshevik Revolution, leaders have used instability to justify repression. Mao's Cultural Revolution led to mass persecution, while Chávez in Venezuela and Marcos in the Philippines eroded democracy through populism and nationalism. Erdoğan in Turkey has similarly weakened democratic safeguards. Modern far-right movements in Europe and the U.S. also exploit economic and cultural fears to justify power centralization. These cases reveal how crises and discontent can be manipulated to entrench authoritarian rule.

This comparative table shows a pattern. Crises serve as an impetus for political realignment, disillusionment about existing elites fuels populist rhetoric, and the erosion of institutional constraints allows leaders to deepen their authority. The role of media—whether traditional or digital—further amplifies these dynamics, enabling charismatic figures to rally mass support while silencing dissenting voices.

Table 3.2: Social Movements and Change Leadership

SOCIAL MOVEMENT	CAUSE OF DISCONTENT & EMERGENT LEADERS	CHANGE PRODUCED
ANTI-APARTHEID MOVEMENT (1948-1994)	Racial segregation, oppression under apartheid; Nelson Mandela, Desmond Tutu, Steve Biko	End of apartheid, multiracial democracy in South Africa
CIVIL RIGHTS MOVEMENT (1950S-1960S)	Racial segregation, systemic discrimination, voter suppression; Martin Luther King Jr., Malcolm X, Rosa Parks	Civil Rights Act, Voting Rights Act, desegregation
ABOLITIONIST MOVEMENT (18TH-19TH C.)	Slavery and human rights abuses; Frederick Douglass, William Lloyd Garrison, Harriet Tubman	Abolition of slavery in the US and globally
WOMEN'S SUFFRAGE MOVEMENT (19TH-20TH C.)	Denial of women's voting rights, gender inequality; Susan B. Anthony, Emmeline Pankhurst, Elizabeth Cady Stanton	Women's suffrage, voting rights expanded globally
LABOR MOVEMENTS (19TH-20TH C.)	Poor working conditions, low wages, lack of labor rights; Cesar Chavez, Samuel Gompers, Mother Jones	Labor laws, minimum wage, workplace safety regulations
ENVIRONMENTAL MOVEMENT (1960S-PRESENT)	Climate change, environmental destruction; Jane Goodall, Greta	Environmental regulations, climate awareness, sustainability policies

	Thunberg, Rachel Carson	
LGBTQ+ Rights Movement (20th-21st C.)	Legal discrimination, lack of civil rights protections; Harvey Milk, Marsha P. Johnson, Christine Jorgensen	LGBTQ+ rights, same-sex marriage legalization, anti-discrimination laws
Bolshevik Revolution (1917)	Czarist rule, wealth inequality, worker exploitation; Vladimir Lenin, Joseph Stalin	Communist Soviet Union, state-controlled economy
National Socialist Movement (1920s-1945)	Economic depression, Treaty of Versailles humiliation; Adolf Hitler	World War II, Holocaust, authoritarian rule
Cultural Revolution (1966-1976)	Ideological corruption, capitalist influence; Mao Zedong	Mass purges, re-education camps, suppression of dissent
Bolivarian Movement (1990s-Present)	Economic inequality, U.S. intervention, dissatisfaction with elites; Hugo Chávez, Nicolás Maduro	Socialist policies, economic crisis, political authoritarianism
Erdoğan's Islamist-Nationalist Movement (2000s-Present)	Secularism, Western interference, economic instability; Recep Tayyip Erdoğan	Erosion of secularism, consolidation of power, media suppression
Brexit Movement (2010s-2020)	Sovereignty, EU regulations, economic migration; Nigel Farage, Boris Johnson	UK withdrawal from EU, economic and political shifts

| Make America Great Again MAGA Movement (2016-Present) | Economic anxiety, job losses, perceived elite corruption; Donald Trump | Erosion of democratic norms, nationalism, anti-immigration policies |
| Bolsonarismo Movement (2018-Present) | Corruption, crime, economic instability, left-wing governance; Jair Bolsonaro | Right-wing governance, deforestation, rollback of civil rights |

These social movements and emerging leaders' cases not only highlights historical precedents but also underscores the contemporary risks of governance transformations driven by discontent movements. As economic inequality, political polarization, and global instability persist, the conditions that have historically given rise to authoritarian and populist leadership remain ever-present. The challenge for democratic resilience lies in addressing the root causes of discontent—through inclusive governance, institutional reforms, and proactive civic engagement—before these movements translate into systemic democratic erosion.

Ultimately, whether a movement leads to progress or authoritarian regression depends on the structures it builds, the leadership it elevates, and the narratives it crafts. Social Movement theories help explain how these dynamics unfold—whether through political opportunity structures (Tarrow, 2011; McAdam, Tarrow, & Tilly, 2001), frame alignment (Snow & Benford, 1988), or economic grievances (Gurr, 1970). Political Opportunity theory suggests that movements gain traction when institutional weaknesses or elite divisions create openings for political challengers (Tarrow, 2011). Frame Alignment theory highlights how leaders and movements shape narratives to resonate with public grievances and mobilize support (Snow & Benford, 1988). Relative Deprivation theory explains how economic grievances, such as unemployment and inequality, fuel discontent and drive mass mobilization (Gurr, 1970). More recently, Cultural Backlash theory (Norris & Inglehart, 2019) has argued that the rise of populist and authoritarian leaders is often a reaction against rapid societal changes in values and identity, particularly among older and more traditionalist segments of the population.

These frameworks collectively provide insights into the mechanisms through which movements empower leaders, shape governance, and either strengthen or erode democratic values. However, one constant remains: in times of widespread discontent, movements have the power to legitimize radical change, sometimes even at the cost of democracy itself. This underscores the importance of understanding and analyzing movements critically—not only as instruments of social change but also as mechanisms through which extreme and risky leaders can gain power.

Leaders Advancing-Receding Governance Progress

History does not follow a straight line; it moves in patterns—sometimes cyclical, sometimes spiral, often rhyming rather than repeating. Scholars have long debated whether governance and leadership evolve through historical cycles or progressive developments shaped by societal conditions. Giambattista Vico (1725) proposed a cyclical theory of history, arguing that civilizations pass through recurring stages of growth, decline, and renewal, often returning to earlier forms in a new guise (*The New Science,* 1744/1999). In contrast, Hegel (1837/1956) and Marx (1867/1992) saw history as a dialectical spiral, where conflicts between old and new forces drive governance toward more advanced forms. A quote often attributed to Mark Twain—that history doesn't repeat itself, but it often rhymes—captures the reality that political structures and leadership dynamics tend to reappear in new contexts, shaped by evolving technological, social, and ideological forces (Collingwood, 1946).

Among the most astute observers of leadership and governance evolution was Niccolò Machiavelli, whose work is often misinterpreted as a mere guide to ruthless and manipulative power-seeking. While in exile after the fall of the Florentine Republic and his imprisonment under the restored Medici regime, Machiavelli wrote both *The Prince* (*Il Principe*, 1532) and *Discourses on Livy* (*Discorsi sopra la prima deca di Tito Livio*, 1531), offering two distinct perspectives on governance. While *The Prince* details how rulers acquire, maintain, and consolidate power, *Discourses on Livy* presents his deeper political philosophy: That republics, when built on institutional balance and civic engagement, are more durable and progressive than autocratic regimes (Machiavelli, 1531/1998). His insights remain relevant today—governance transitions are shaped not only by leaders' ability to manipulate, adapt, and seize historical moments but also by the strength of institutions and citizen participation (Skinner, 1978).

Just as Machiavelli explored power and institutions in political leadership, Adam Smith examined governance through the lens of economic and moral philosophy. His contributions are often reduced to a narrow interpretation centered on his book, *The Wealth of Nations* (1776), neglecting his earlier work, *The Theory of Moral Sentiments* (1759), where he emphasized the ethical and social foundations necessary for a just society. Smith recognized that markets alone do not ensure equitable governance; rather, economic and political institutions must be grounded in moral considerations and social cohesion (Smith, 1759/2002). The frequent misinterpretation of his ideas reflects a broader issue in governance evolution—leaders and policymakers often prioritize economic efficiency and power consolidation without integrating ethical principles or civic engagement. This disconnect has historically hindered the transition from extractive to inclusive institutions, reinforcing authoritarian control rather than fostering democratic participation. Understanding governance leadership requires moving beyond isolated economic frameworks to recognize the interplay between power, morality, and institutional design (Sen, 2017; Acemoglu & Robinson, 2012).

Governance evolution follows recognizable patterns, oscillating between authoritarianism and democracy, centralized and decentralized rule, and exclusion and inclusion. However, as Daron Acemoglu and James Robinson argue in *Why Nations Fail* (2012), these transitions are not merely the product of historical determinism or economic inevitability—they are shaped by the institutional choices and strategic decisions of leaders who either reinforce extractive institutions that concentrate power and wealth or build inclusive institutions that enable broader political participation and economic prosperity.

Acemoglu further explored these dynamics in *Economic Origins of Dictatorship and Democracy* (2006), where he analyzed the strategic interactions between elites and the broader society in shaping governance evolution. He argues that democracy does not emerge automatically from economic development but rather through power struggles where leaders either concede reforms to prevent revolution or suppress democratic demands to maintain control. Leaders facing institutional pressures make decisions that either push governance toward greater inclusion or cause democratic backsliding into autocracy. This interplay between elite bargaining, mass mobilization, and institutional resilience explains why some countries transition more successfully toward democracy while others remain in cycles of repression.

In *The Narrow Corridor: States, Societies, and the Fate of Liberty* (2019), Acemoglu expands his argument by emphasizing that stable democracies emerge when there is a delicate balance between state strength and societal mobilization. He introduces the concept of the "Red Queen Effect", in which states and societies must continuously evolve in mutual contestation to prevent the dominance of either a despotic state or a weak, fragmented political system. Leaders play a crucial role in maintaining this equilibrium, as they either strengthen institutions to balance governance power or tilt the system toward autocracy by weakening civil society and democratic constraints.

Acemoglu's most recent work, *Power and Progress: Our Thousand-Year Struggle Over Technology and Prosperity* (2023), further connects governance evolution to technological change, arguing that technological advancements do not inherently lead to shared prosperity. Instead, leaders and institutions shape how technology is distributed—whether it is used to empower broad social progress or to reinforce elite control and widen inequality. Governance, therefore, is not just about political arrangements but also economic and technological structures, where leaders either harness progress to build inclusive institutions or exploit innovations to consolidate authoritarian power.

Thus, governance shifts—whether from monarchical rule to constitutional democracies, from male-dominated societies to inclusive political representation, or from extractive economies to regenerative models—depend on whether leaders choose to open political and economic opportunities to broader segments of society or suppress change to maintain their dominance. Unlike Fukuyama's (2011) perspective on the gradual consolidation of state institutions, Acemoglu underscores that governance progress is often a contested, high-stakes struggle, where leaders navigate between resistance, reform, and revolutionary change—with the outcomes shaping not just governance systems but the long-term trajectory of national development.

Leadership plays a decisive role in the evolution of governance, shaping whether societies move toward greater inclusion, stability, and innovation or descend into oppression and stagnation. Leaders can be broadly classified into four key types based on their approach to power and governance: **Authoritarians,** who consolidate control, often at the expense of political freedoms and institutional integrity; **Revolutionaries,** who overthrow old systems to establish new governance structures, sometimes leading to progress and other times to instability; **Compromisers,** who seek to balance competing forces to ensure stability and negotiated reforms; and **Reformers,** who drive positive change from within existing institutions, expanding rights, participation, and accountability.

This classification helps us understand the pivotal role of leadership in governance transitions, whether in the formation of empires, the collapse of totalitarian regimes, the expansion of democracy, or the redefinition of economic and environmental policies. Leaders can act as catalysts for transformation or obstacles to progress, determining whether societies move toward justice and sustainability or remain entrenched in cycles of exploitation and conflict.

Table 3.3 provides an overview of historical and contemporary leaders across these four categories, illustrating how their leadership styles influenced governance evolution in different contexts.

Table 3.3: Leaders' Response to Events

LEADER CLASSIFICATION	GOVERNANCE EVENT	LEADERSHIP CHARACTERISTIC
JULIUS CAESAR (AUTHORITARIAN)	End of the Roman Republic and rise of the Roman Empire	Military strategy, political manipulation, governance consolidation
ADOLF HITLER (AUTHORITARIAN)	Weimar Republic collapse and establishment of Nazi Germany	Propagandist, expansionist, totalitarian control
JOSEPH STALIN (AUTHORITARIAN)	Consolidation of power and creation of totalitarian USSR	Industrialization, purges, totalitarian rule
XI JINPING (AUTHORITARIAN)	Expansion of authoritarian governance and state surveillance in China	Technocratic authoritarianism, centralized control, economic expansion
VLADIMIR PUTIN (AUTHORITARIAN)	Centralization of power in Russia, crackdown on dissent, and foreign intervention	Hybrid authoritarianism, nationalist policies, state control over media
FRANCISCO FRANCO (AUTHORITARIAN)	Spanish Civil War victory and establishment of a right-wing dictatorship	Right-wing nationalism, military authoritarianism, centralized rule

AUGUSTO PINOCHET (AUTHORITARIAN)	Military coup in Chile and establishment of an authoritarian neoliberal state	Authoritarian capitalism, suppression of opposition, economic reform
GEORGE WASHINGTON (REVOLUTIONARY)	American Revolution and establishment of U.S. democracy	Military leadership, institutional founder, democratic governance
VLADIMIR LENIN (REVOLUTIONARY)	Bolshevik Revolution and creation of the Soviet Union	Revolutionary, ideological leadership, centralized economic planning
CHE GUEVARA (REVOLUTIONARY)	Cuban Revolution and guerrilla warfare to overthrow Batista's regime	Revolutionary tactics, socialist ideology, military strategy
MAHATMA GANDHI (REVOLUTIONARY)	Indian independence movement and nonviolent resistance against British rule	Moral leadership, nonviolent resistance, strategic mobilization
ANGELA MERKEL (COMPROMISER)	Stabilization of European Union during economic and refugee crises	Consensus-building, negotiation, crisis management
LEE KUAN YEW (COMPROMISER)	Economic transformation of Singapore from a small city-state to a global power	Technocratic governance, strategic economic planning, legalistic approach
KOFI ANNAN (COMPROMISER)	UN diplomacy, peacekeeping efforts, and global governance initiatives	Global peacekeeping, diplomatic negotiation, multilateralism

JOHN F. KENNEDY (COMPROMISER)	Civil rights support, Cold War diplomacy, and space race leadership	Charismatic leadership, crisis management, international collaboration
NELSON MANDELA (COMPROMISER)	Transition from apartheid to multiracial democracy in South Africa	Reconciliation, democratic transition, anti-apartheid activism
THEODORE ROOSEVELT (REFORMER)	Progressive Era reforms, antitrust laws, and expansion of U.S. federal power	Trust-busting, progressive policies, environmental conservation
ELLEN JOHNSON SIRLEAF (REFORMER)	Post-civil war reconstruction and governance reform in Liberia	Rebuilding national institutions, gender inclusivity, anti-corruption
BARACK OBAMA (REFORMER)	Affordable Care Act, economic recovery post-2008 crisis, and diplomacy	Healthcare reform, economic diplomacy, social justice initiatives
FRANKLIN D. ROOSEVELT (REFORMER)	New Deal reforms and expansion of federal government during the Great Depression	Progressive social policies, economic reform, crisis leadership

Why Leaders Should Promote Evolution

Evolution is a fundamental principle that governs not only biological systems but also social, technological, economic, and political structures. It represents continuous adaptation, innovation, and progress in response to challenges. While setbacks and resistance are common, history has demonstrated that humanity possesses an extraordinary ability to evolve and overcome obstacles. Leadership—whether in government, business, or civil society—plays a crucial role in either accelerating or obstructing this evolution. Forward-thinking leaders must recognize that progress is not only inevitable but also necessary for long-term stability, prosperity, and sustainability. However, governance and leadership must not be mistaken for corporate management. Societies do not function like businesses, nor can technological advances alone resolve the complexities of human life. Governance must be a dynamic and inclusive process that balances economic efficiency with social well-being, scientific advancements with ethical considerations, and individual leadership with collective responsibility.

In biological evolution, species survive by adapting to their environments, developing new traits, and refining their survival strategies. Charles Darwin's theory of natural selection demonstrated that the most adaptable species—not necessarily the strongest or fittest—are the ones that persist. Similarly, in the world of medicine, the evolution of antibiotic resistance in bacteria illustrates both the power of adaptation and the dangers of stagnation. The overuse of antibiotics has driven bacterial evolution in ways that now threaten human health, requiring medical research and policy innovation to stay ahead of emerging superbugs (Davies & Davies, 2010). This principle of adaptation applies across all sectors; leaders who fail to recognize the necessity of change risk catastrophic consequences. However, just as biological evolution is not a linear or predetermined path, neither is societal progress. Leadership must foster structures that allow for adaptation rather than rigid, top-down systems that prevent responsiveness to change.

Social and cultural evolution is equally evident throughout history. Societies have progressively moved toward greater inclusion, equality, and democratic participation, though not without resistance. The abolition of slavery, the expansion of women's rights, and the global fight against apartheid and segregation illustrate how once-radical ideas eventually became foundational to modern governance and human rights (Darity, 2008). The Civil Rights Movement in the United States, for example, faced violent opposition, yet its persistence led to legal reforms such as the Civil Rights Act of 1964 and the Voting Rights Act of 1965, fundamentally reshaping American democracy. Similarly, South Africa's transition from apartheid to a multiracial democracy, led by Nelson Mandela, demonstrates how societies can evolve beyond exclusionary policies and toward inclusive governance. Although, these changes did not occur automatically or through market forces alone—they required governance structures that promoted human dignity over economic expediency.

Technological evolution has been one of the most transformative forces in human history, reshaping societies from the printing press to the internet. The transition from fossil fuels to renewable energy shows how technology drives economic and environmental change. Countries investing in clean energy, such as Denmark and Germany, are not only reducing carbon emissions but also positioning themselves as leaders in the emerging green economy (Jacobsson & Bergek, 2004). However, as Acemoglu and Johnson (2023) argue, unchecked technological progress can lead to technocratic dominance, where economic and political power becomes concentrated among elites who control innovation, limiting broader prosperity. A society governed primarily by technological efficiency—without democratic oversight, institutional balance, and inclusive policies—risks exacerbating inequality, undermining labor rights, and reducing individual freedoms. While artificial intelligence, automation, and digital platforms promise increased efficiency, they also raise ethical concerns about labor displacement, surveillance, and misinformation. Leadership must therefore resist the fallacy of technocratic inevitability, integrating innovation within a framework of responsible governance that prioritizes equity, accessibility, and long-term sustainability over short-term economic gains (Friedman, 2019).

Economic evolution follows similar patterns, with shifts from localized economies to industrial production and now toward digital and knowledge-based economies. The 2008 global financial crisis exposed weaknesses in deregulated financial markets, leading to increased scrutiny and regulatory reforms designed to prevent future collapses (Stiglitz, 2010). Similarly, the growing emphasis on corporate social responsibility (CSR) and environmental, social, and governance (ESG) factors reflects a shift from purely profit-driven models to more sustainable economic approaches. The rise of the circular economy—where businesses prioritize resource efficiency, waste reduction, and product life extension—demonstrates an evolution in how we conceptualize economic growth (Stahel, 2016). However, businesses alone cannot be the sole drivers of social responsibility. While some corporations have embraced ESG principles, others continue to prioritize short-term profits over long-term well-being, engaging in greenwashing or exploitative labor practices. The responsibility of governance is to ensure that businesses do not merely evolve to remain competitive but evolve to align with broader social and environmental needs.

Governance and political evolution have also been central to human progress. While authoritarian regimes persist in certain regions, global trends show a long-term shift toward participatory governance, transparency, and human rights. The fall of colonial empires and the emergence of independent nations in the 20th century reveal a political evolution toward self-governance and autonomy. Similarly, the collapse of the Soviet Union and the subsequent democratization of Eastern European states illustrate how rigid, top-down political systems often fail to sustain long-term stability (Huntington, 1991). Even in the face of democratic backsliding in some nations, movements for government accountability and citizen participation continue to gain strength. This suggests that governance must be a process of continuous study and adaptation, where leaders are held accountable, and systems remain flexible to the evolving needs of their people.

At the same time, the growing interdependence of nations has necessitated the development of multilateral institutions and international norms to regulate global relations and address collective challenges. Institutions such as the United Nations, the European Union, the World Trade Organization, and environmental agreements like the Paris Accord reflect the increasing recognition that no nation operates in isolation. Multilateral governance mechanisms provide frameworks for cooperation, conflict resolution, and the enforcement of global responsibilities, particularly in areas such as environmental protection, human rights, and economic stability (Keohane, 2020; Sachs et al., 2022). As the effects of climate change, resource depletion, and technological advancements shape future global dynamics, governance structures must evolve to uphold not only the rights and needs of present populations but also the well-being of future generations (United Nations, 2021). The responsibility to create sustainable policies and ethical leadership in international relations is no longer a choice but a necessity for long-term planetary stability. Recent analyses emphasize the critical role of multilateral development banks in financing climate initiatives, calling for substantial increases in international climate finance to meet global warming targets (World Bank, 2023). Additionally, the rise of populism presents significant challenges to multilateralism and global governance, requiring concerted efforts to promote inclusive and democratic solutions (Rachman, 2021; Zürn, 2022).

While evolutionary dynamics are evident across governance, business, and society, it is crucial to recognize that these fields operate under distinct principles and objectives. Governance is fundamentally about stewardship of the public good, ensuring that essential services, rights, and infrastructure are safeguarded and accessible to all. It is not merely an extension of business management, nor can societal progress be reduced to market efficiency alone. While efficiency—the ability to minimize costs and maximize outputs—is often championed in private-sector management, governance must prioritize effectiveness, ensuring that policies and institutions uphold justice, sustainability, and the common good over time. Public systems must serve broad societal needs rather than be subjected to cost-cutting imperatives that may undermine long-term well-being.

The growing trend of privatization, often justified under the banner of efficiency, has profound implications for the public good. As Cohen and Mikaelian (2021) argue in *The Privatization of Everything*, this shift risks transforming public services from rights into commodities, limiting access based on profit motives rather than collective need. Privatization can erode democratic accountability, replacing public oversight with corporate governance structures that prioritize shareholder returns over equitable service provision. Essential sectors such as education, healthcare, and infrastructure—historically managed to ensure universal access—are increasingly subjected to market-driven models that may lead to unequal access, service deterioration, and a loss of public trust. Efficiency in the private sector often means cost-cutting, outsourcing, and streamlining, but in governance, such an approach can have detrimental effects by undermining public services, disenfranchising marginalized communities, and weakening institutional resilience in times of crisis.

However, it is also important to recognize that the private sector itself is evolving in response to growing societal and global responsibilities. Corporations are increasingly acknowledging their role in fostering the common good through corporate social, environmental and global responsibility. The shift toward stakeholder capitalism suggests that businesses are moving beyond pure profit motives to consider long-term societal value. This trend, while promising, does not negate the irreplaceable role of government in ensuring equity, justice, and sustainability. Unlike businesses, whose priorities can shift with market forces, governance must remain a deliberate and accountable steward of the public good, ensuring that economic, social, and environmental protections are not contingent on corporate goodwill alone.

Table 3.4 distinguishes governance leadership dynamics from business leadership dynamics, highlighting these critical differences. While both sectors evolve and adapt, their core priorities, decision-making structures, and measures of success remain distinct. Recognizing these distinctions is essential to prevent the erosion of public trust and to ensure that privatization, where it occurs, does not undermine the fundamental responsibility of governance: to serve all citizens equitably, protect human rights, and sustain the collective well-being of present and future generations. At the same time, business leaders must continue aligning their operations with broader social and environmental responsibilities, ensuring that economic activity supports rather than supplants the public good.

Table 3.4: Government and Business Leadership Dynamics

Aspect	Government Leadership → Privatization Dynamics	Business Leadership → Responsibility Dynamics
Primary Goal	Serve public good, stability, equity, justice → Increasingly outsourcing services to private entities	Profitability → Integrating social responsibility, sustainability
Decision-Making	Democratic, participatory, accountable to citizens → Influenced by private sector partnerships and lobbying	Executive-driven → Stakeholder governance, ethical leadership
Responsibility	Social welfare, public services, economic/legal stability → Growing private sector involvement in infrastructure, healthcare, and education	Competitive products/services → Corporate citizenship, ESG integration
Time Horizon	Long-term, intergenerational planning → Shifting toward short term wins influenced by private sector logic	Short-term financial performance → Balancing immediate gains and long-term value
Funding Source	Taxes, public revenue, regulatory frameworks → Increasing reliance on private partnerships, outsourcing, and user fees	Private investments → Hybrid models (impact investing, green finance, social enterprise)

MEASURE OF SUCCESS	Public trust, economic stability, quality of life → increasingly measured by efficiency and cost-cutting	Profitability, shareholder returns → Impact metrics (sustainability, social impact)
RESPONSE TO CRISIS	Public safety, disaster response, economic protection → Increase reliance and collaboration with private entities	Cost-cutting, risk management → Corporate social responsibility, community resilience
ACCOUNTABILITY	Citizen elections, legal oversight, transparency → Rising corporate influence in policy decisions	Shareholders, boards → Workers, communities, global regulations

Despite this broad pattern of evolution, progress is not linear. Setbacks may occur, often fueled by reactionary forces that resist change to maintain power or economic advantage. Scientific discoveries have historically been met with opposition, as seen in the persecution of Galileo for advocating heliocentrism. Similarly, social resistance to progress is evident in ongoing struggles for gender equality and LGBTQ+ rights, where gains are often followed by pushbacks. However, history demonstrates that such opposition eventually gives way to broader acceptance and systemic change. For instance, same-sex marriage, once unthinkable in many countries, is now legally recognized in over 30 nations, reflecting an evolution in societal values (Badgett, 2020). These advancements are not simply the result of market forces or individual leadership but rather the result of governance structures that enable the institutionalization of new rights and protections.

Governance and leadership, therefore, must embrace evolution as a guiding principle rather than a disruptive force to be feared. Leaders must actively promote rather than hinder progress, recognizing that adaptation is essential for survival—not just in biology but also in governance, business, and civil society. Those who resist change risk irrelevance, as seen in the downfall of companies and governments that failed to respond to shifting economic and technological landscapes. Governments that embrace innovation and reform tend to be more resilient, while those that cling to outdated models often face economic and social crises. Scandinavian nations, for example, have successfully balanced market economies with social welfare, demonstrating how adaptive governance can lead to both economic growth and social equity. In contrast, countries that resist democratic reforms and global cooperation often experience internal instability and economic isolation.

Ultimately, no single sector—government, business, or technology—can provide all the answers to humanity's most pressing challenges. Business alone cannot be the solution, as societies require governance structures that prioritize collective well-being over corporate interests. Technology alone cannot be the solution, as ethical considerations must guide its application in human life. Leaders alone cannot find solutions in isolation, as citizens must actively engage in shaping their societies. Instead of expecting governance to operate like a business, or technology to replace human decision-making, leadership should focus on fostering collaboration, innovation, and inclusive governance structures that ensure that evolution—whether social, technological, or economic—leads to a more just and sustainable future for all.

Governance as Dynamic System

Throughout this chapter, we have argued that governance is not a static construct but an evolving process that mirrors the values, challenges, and aspirations of societies over time. Leaders engaged in governance transformation must recognize that their actions are not isolated but rather part of a larger historical continuum—one that is shaped by the past and extends far into the future. Transformation does not happen overnight, nor is it ever truly complete. Instead, governance is a dynamic system that requires leaders to think beyond immediate political cycles and short-term gains, embracing a broader, more sustainable vision of progress.

Movements play a crucial role in shaping governance by empowering leaders who either foster societal progress or erode democratic values. Historically, movements like the Civil Rights Movement, the Women's Suffrage Movement, and the Anti-Apartheid Movement have empowered leaders committed to justice, human rights, and inclusive governance. These movements produced figures like Martin Luther King Jr., Nelson Mandela, and Emmeline Pankhurst, whose leadership transformed societies toward greater equity and democracy. However, history also demonstrates how movements driven by economic discontent, cultural grievances, or nationalist fervor can legitimize authoritarian rulers, as seen in the rise of Adolf Hitler through the Nazi movement, Mao Zedong's leadership in the Cultural Revolution, and more recently, Jair Bolsonaro's political rise through Bolsonarismo in Brazil. In these cases, movements became mechanisms for consolidating power, suppressing dissent, and reshaping governance structures in ways that weakened democratic institutions and eroded civil liberties.

This dual potential of movements highlights the responsibility of civic society, policymakers, and institutions to critically engage with and guide movements toward democratic resilience rather than authoritarian regression. Governance, as a dynamic system, is influenced not just by individual leaders but by the collective forces that sustain their legitimacy. Whether movements produce leaders who advance democracy or dismantle it depends on how societies channel their collective discontent, aspirations, and demands for change. As history has shown, governance is never neutral—it is either evolving toward greater inclusion and justice or regressing into control and suppression. Recognizing this reality is key to ensuring that movements remain forces for positive transformation rather than an impetus for authoritarianism.

Machiavelli reminds us, "Whosoever desires constant success must change his conduct with the times" (Machiavelli, 1532/2003). Indeed, true leadership is about adaptation—understanding the shifting tides of society and shaping institutions that remain relevant and just. Leaders who resist change risk governing in ways that become obsolete or even harmful. However, transformation is not only about responding to the present; it must also be guided by a principled vision for the future. The Native American principle of thinking seven generations ahead provides a powerful ethical and strategic framework for governance transformation. This long-term perspective challenges us to weigh the consequences of our decisions not only for today's stakeholders but for those who will inherit the systems we shape. As Chief Oren Lyons of the Onondaga Nation explained, "We are looking ahead, as is one of the first mandates given us as chiefs, to make sure that every decision we make relates to the welfare and well-being of the seventh generation to come" (Lyons, 1980).

This intergenerational awareness requires humility—an acknowledgment that transformation is not the work of a single leader or administration but a process of continuous adaptation and improvement. John F. Kennedy aptly put it, "Leadership and learning are indispensable to each other" (Kennedy, 1963). The ability to learn from history, from society, and from the people one serves is crucial in shaping governance that is truly inclusive and effective. Lao Tzu's wisdom captures this well: "To lead people, walk behind them" (Lao Tzu, trans. 1972). Governance transformations must be participatory, empowering communities and institutions to co-create the change they need. The most enduring governance reforms are those that are co-designed, grounded in shared values, and adaptable to the evolving needs of society.

At the heart of governance transformation is a personal commitment to change. Mahatma Gandhi famously stated, "Be the change that you wish to see in the world" (Gandhi, 1913/1995). Leaders must embody the principles they advocate for, recognizing that transformation begins with the values and integrity of those who guide the process. Historian Yuval Noah Harari suggests in *21 Lessons for the 21st Century*, "Change is the only constant in history. Never before has humanity needed to adapt as quickly as it does today" (Harari, 2018, p. 55). The accelerating pace of change in governance, technology, and global challenges requires leaders to cultivate both wisdom and foresight. We need leaders that recognize governance is an act of stewardship and that their role is not only to manage the present but to prepare the future for those who will follow.

PART 2
DECODING FASCIST DYNAMICS

| 4 |

DECODING FASCISM

> *"It took the Nazis one month, three weeks, two days, eight hours and 40 minutes to dismantle a constitutional republic."*
>
> — Illinois Governor JB Pritzker, February 19, 2025

The term "fascism" derives from the Latin word "fasces" meaning a bundle of rods bound together around an axe, symbolizing strength through unity and the authority of the state (Paxton, 2005). This ancient Roman emblem, representing collective power and justice, was later incorporated into the iconography of Mussolini's regime as a deliberate link to Italy's imperial past. Mussolini sought to "Make Italy Great Again" by reviving the grandeur of the Roman Empire, positioning his leadership as a modern imperator who would restore Italy's dominance among the world's great powers. He envisioned a new Italian empire that would reclaim its place among other colonizing nations, using Roman imagery and rhetoric to justify expansionist ambitions in Africa and the Mediterranean. The "fasces" also appears in the U.S. House of Representatives as a nod to republican ideals of governance, but in Italy, it was repurposed as a symbol of absolute authority. Before Mussolini's movement, the term *fasci* had a different connotation in Sicily, where the Fasci Siciliani (1891–1894) emerged as a grassroots movement advocating for the rights of farmers and laborers against oppressive landlords. However, Mussolini transformed the concept into a nationalist and militarized ideology, harnessing the postwar crisis to present himself as *L'Uomo della Provvidenza*—the man of providence (as Pope Pios XI called him)—a leader sent to restore Italy's strength and imperial destiny (Fattorini, 2011). His rise was not merely political but deeply symbolic, appealing to a population seeking order, revival, and a return to a glorious past that he promised to resurrect.

To better recognize and understand the dynamics of fascism in today's authoritarian leadership practices, we must first examine how fascism emerged in Italy, what it fought against, and what it proposed. According to Robert Paxton (2005), "officially, Fascism was born in Milan on Sunday, March 23, 1919, when more than a hundred persons, including war veterans, syndicalists who had supported the war, and Futurist intellectuals, plus some reporters and the merely curious, gathered in the meeting room of the Milan Industrial and Commercial Alliance, overlooking the Piazza San Sepolcro, to 'declare war against socialism... because it has opposed nationalism'" (p. 5). In this moment, Mussolini founded the *Fasci di Combattimento*—fraternities of combat—which would evolve into a totalitarian movement that shaped Italy's political trajectory for the next two decades.

Fascism in Italy did not simply emerge as a political ideology; it was deeply tied to the fascination with Mussolini as the man of providence, a leader who projected strength, decisiveness, and destiny. In the aftermath of World War I, Italy faced economic turmoil, social upheaval, and political fragmentation. The liberal government was perceived as weak, unable to unify the country or address the rising tensions between workers and industrial elites. At the same time, socialism and communism gained momentum, fueling fears of class conflict and revolution among the middle and upper classes. Mussolini positioned fascism as the antidote to these crises, rejecting liberal democracy for its inefficacy, socialism for its class struggle, and laissez-faire capitalism for its instability (Paxton, 2005). However, his appeal was not merely ideological; it was personal. He crafted an image of himself as the savior of Italy, a leader destined to restore order and national greatness. As Scurati (2022) describes, Mussolini did not seize power through ideological persuasion alone but through the cult of his persona, becoming a figure upon whom Italians projected their hopes and fears.

One of the core targets of fascism was liberalism, which emphasized individual rights, democracy, and free markets. Fascists viewed liberal democratic institutions as weak and ineffective in maintaining national unity. The postwar Italian government, a liberal democracy, struggled with political fragmentation and economic crises, which Mussolini exploited by promising strong leadership and order. Unlike liberalism, which values political pluralism and free speech, fascism suppressed opposition, centralized power under a single leader *(Il Duce)*, and prioritized the state over individual freedoms (Gentile, 2005a). While some elements of free-market economics persisted under fascism, economic policies were subordinated to nationalistic and militaristic goals, with the state directing industries in ways that aligned with its expansionist ambitions.

At the same time, fascism also positioned itself as a direct adversary of socialism and communism, particularly in Italy, where socialist movements were gaining strength. The rise of leftist labor unions, peasant uprisings, and the Italian Socialist Party (PSI) led to fears among landowners, industrialists, and conservatives that Italy was on the verge of a communist revolution. Mussolini, a former socialist himself, rejected Marxism's class-based struggle and instead promoted a corporatist model, where labor and industry were coordinated under state control rather than abolished. Unlike socialism, which sought to eliminate class distinctions through wealth redistribution, fascism preserved existing class structures but integrated them under a state-led system that purported to balance the interests of workers and employers. In practice, however, fascist Italy crushed labor unions, suppressed strikes, and promoted nationalist rhetoric to replace class identity with loyalty to the nation-state (De Felice, 1995).

While fascism shared some skepticism toward capitalism, particularly in its laissez-faire form, it did not seek to dismantle private enterprise as socialism did. Instead, it promoted corporatism, a system where industries, workers, and the state worked together to serve national interests. Under Mussolini, the Italian government heavily intervened in the economy, establishing state-controlled syndicates to regulate production while still allowing private ownership. Unlike capitalism, which thrives on free markets and competition, fascism placed economic activity under strict state oversight, prioritizing military expansion and autarky (economic self-sufficiency). However, Mussolini still relied on industrial elites and business leaders, ensuring that capitalism, though constrained, remained an integral part of the fascist system (Eatwell, 2011).

Another fundamental aspect of fascism was its rejection of pacifism and internationalism. The ideology glorified war and imperial conquest, directly opposing movements that sought peace or international cooperation, such as the League of Nations. Mussolini's Italy pursued aggressive expansionism, invading Ethiopia in 1935 and later aligning with Nazi Germany in World War II (Kallis, 2000). Unlike liberalism and socialism, which advocate for diplomatic engagement or class solidarity across national boundaries, fascism upheld the idea of national superiority and used violence as a means of strengthening the state.

At its core, fascism was authoritarian and anti-pluralistic, eliminating all forms of political opposition. While other authoritarian regimes also concentrated power, fascism was unique in its emphasis on mass mobilization, propaganda, and the creation of a cult of personality around the leader. Mussolini controlled the press, education, and even cultural life to instill fascist ideology into every aspect of society (Gentile, 1997). Unlike traditional monarchies or military dictatorships that merely maintained order, fascist regimes sought to reshape society through indoctrination and totalitarian control. The Fascist Party became the singular force in Italy's political system, and the OVRA (Organization for Vigilance and Repression of Anti-Fascism), Mussolini's secret police, ensured that dissent was swiftly suppressed.

Understanding the similarities and differences between historical fascist ideologies and their reactions to other political movements of the time is crucial for recognizing the patterns of authoritarianism that persist today. Fascism, particularly under Mussolini, did not emerge in isolation—it developed in response to and in conflict with competing ideologies such as liberal democracy, socialism, communism, and capitalism. Each of these systems represented a different vision for political and economic organization, and Mussolini's approach was shaped by both opposition to and strategic alignment with elements of these ideologies.

Table 4.1 provides a comparative framework that examines how fascism interacted with these competing systems during Mussolini's era. For instance, while fascism rejected liberal democracy's emphasis on individual rights and political pluralism, it borrowed aspects of its economic structure to accommodate corporate and elite interests. Similarly, fascist regimes fiercely opposed socialism and communism, viewing class-based movements as existential threats, yet they often adopted state interventionist policies to consolidate power and appeal to the working class. Additionally, while capitalism was tolerated and even encouraged under Mussolini in a controlled form, it was subordinated to the interests of the state, aligning with the fascist ideal of a strong, centralized government overseeing economic activity.

Table 4.1: Comparing Mussolini's Fascism with Other Systems

SYSTEM	CORE FEATURES	COMPARISON
LIBERALISM	Individual rights, democracy, free markets, limited government	Opposes personal freedoms, democracy, political pluralism; Mussolini dismantled democratic institutions, suppressed press, banned opposition parties

SOCIALISM	Collective ownership, economic equality, welfare state	Maintains class hierarchies and private property; Mussolini suppressed socialism, banned unions, promoted corporatist policies
COMMUNISM	Total state control of economy, abolition of private property, class struggle	Keeps capitalism intact under state control; Mussolini crushed communist opposition, promoted nationalism as alternative
CAPITALISM	Free markets, private property, profit motive	Restricts markets, emphasizes nationalism over profit; Mussolini implemented state-controlled economy but allowed industrial elite power
AUTHORITARIANISM	Strong centralized power, limited political freedoms	Emphasizes nationalism, militarism, mass mobilization uniquely; Mussolini ruled as a dictator, used secret police, controlled media
SOCIAL NATIONALISM (NAZISM)	Extreme nationalism, racial purity, totalitarian control	Focused on state power vs. Nazism's racial emphasis; Mussolini eventually aligned with Nazi racial policies
PACIFISM & INTERNATIONALISM	Advocacy for peace, diplomacy, global cooperation	Promoted war, military expansion; Mussolini withdrew from League of Nations, invaded Ethiopia, allied with Nazi Germany
POLITICAL PLURALISM	Multiple parties, free elections, democratic governance	Enforced single-party state; Mussolini banned opposition, established totalitarianism, controlled public discourse

Fascism positioned itself in relation to other major political and economic systems during Mussolini's time, highlighting both ideological clashes and strategic alignments. Fascism emerged as a reactionary response to liberal democracy, socialism, and perceived economic instability. Combining intense nationalism with authoritarian governance, it explicitly rejected individual freedoms and class-based revolutionary ideologies. Unlike communism, fascism permitted some private enterprise but kept businesses under strict state oversight, subordinating economic activity to the interests of the regime.

Recognizing these historical interactions is essential for understanding the evolution of authoritarianism in modern contexts. While today's authoritarian leaders do not necessarily follow Mussolini's exact model, they employ similar strategies, selectively adopting elements from different ideological frameworks to justify their rule and maintain control. For example, contemporary right-wing populist leaders, while often aligned with free-market policies, also engage in nationalist economic interventions reminiscent of fascist corporatism. Likewise, modern autocrats frequently exploit nationalist rhetoric while strategically suppressing leftist movements that challenge economic and social inequality. These historical parallels demonstrate how fascist and authoritarian tendencies adapt to different political and economic landscapes, making it crucial to remain vigilant against the resurgence of illiberal governance under new guises.

Italian fascism was built on an authoritarian structure that fused nationalism with an aggressive suppression of dissent, prioritizing order and unity over individual freedoms. However, Mussolini's rise to power was not solely the result of political or economic instability. As Scurati (2022) emphasizes, it was also driven by Italy's collective yearning for a leader who embodied strength, destiny, and inevitability. Mussolini's appeal was not just ideological but deeply psychological—he was perceived as a messianic figure, a man who could restore Italy's lost grandeur and lead the nation to renewed prominence. This widespread public fascination with Mussolini allowed him to consolidate power, erode democratic institutions, and establish a regime where personal loyalty to the leader replaced democratic accountability. The enduring legacy of Mussolini's cult of personality serves as a stark warning. When societies invest their faith in charismatic leaders rather than in democratic principles, authoritarianism finds fertile ground to take root and flourish. As Francesco Filippi (2020) argues, many Italians have yet to reckon with the fascist past, allowing its cultural roots and symbols to persist and resurface in contemporary society, often in subtle but troubling ways.

The Recurrent Nature of Authoritarianism

Fascism is often dismissed as a historical aberration, a dark chapter confined to the 20th century. However, authoritarianism is not an anomaly—it is a recurring force that emerges in different forms across time and societies. The mechanisms of fascist rule—centralized power, suppression of dissent, and militarized nationalism—are not relics of the past but persistent threats that adapt to modern political landscapes. Whether through autocratic leaders, extreme nationalist movements, or creeping state control, the resurgence of fascist tendencies serves as a stark reminder that democracy is never guaranteed.

The recurrence of fascism and authoritarianism is not random; it follows a predictable pattern where charismatic strongmen exploit moments of crisis to consolidate power. Throughout history, fascist regimes have not emerged in a vacuum but have capitalized on periods of economic instability, social unrest, political dysfunction, and national humiliation to justify their rule. These crises create a climate of fear, frustration, and disillusionment with democratic governance, allowing authoritarian leaders to position themselves as the only viable solution to restoring national stability and strength. Here are some historical correlations between crises and the rise of fascist and authoritarian regimes:

Mussolini and Post-WWI Chaos – Benito Mussolini took advantage of Italy's post-World War I turmoil, marked by economic depression, widespread strikes, and violent class struggles between socialists and conservatives. Italy's parliamentary democracy appeared weak and ineffective, fueling the perception that the country needed a strong, decisive leader. Mussolini's Blackshirts used violence to crush leftist opposition, while his rhetoric of restoring Italy's imperial greatness gained traction among disillusioned Italians. On October 28-31, 1922, he staged the March on Rome, coercing King Victor Emmanuel III into appointing him as prime minister—an event that marked the beginning of fascist rule in Italy (Foot, 2022)

Hitler and the Great Depression – Germany's humiliation after World War I, exacerbated by the harsh terms of the Treaty of Versailles, created fertile ground for the Nazi Party. The hyperinflation crisis of the 1920s, followed by the Great Depression, devastated the economy and left millions unemployed. Weimar democracy was seen as weak and chaotic, leading many Germans to seek an alternative. Hitler, leveraging his propaganda machine and paramilitary SA (Brownshirts), positioned himself as the only leader capable of restoring Germany's strength. In 1933, after the Reichstag Fire, Hitler exploited the national emergency to push through the Enabling Act, granting him dictatorial powers and dismantling German democracy (Baranowski, et al. 2018).

Franco and the Spanish Civil War – In Spain, General Francisco Franco used the political instability of the Second Spanish Republic as a pretext to launch a military coup in 1936. The Spanish Civil War (1936–1939) became a battleground between fascist, communist, and democratic forces. With the support of Nazi Germany and Fascist Italy, Franco's forces ultimately triumphed, establishing a nationalist dictatorship that would last until his death in 1975. Franco's rule demonstrated how fascist regimes could emerge from civil conflict by suppressing opposition through mass executions, censorship, and political persecution.

Pinochet and the Coup in Chile – In 1973, General Augusto Pinochet exploited Chile's economic and political crisis to overthrow the democratically elected socialist president, Salvador Allende. With U.S. backing, Pinochet justified his coup as necessary to prevent Chile from falling into communism. His regime suspended civil liberties, murdered political opponents, and ruled through fear and repression. Like earlier fascist leaders, he used national security threats as an excuse to justify authoritarian control.

Gaddafi and the "Permanent Revolution" – Libyan dictator Muammar Gaddafi seized power in 1969 following a military coup against King Idris. Exploiting anti-colonial sentiment and economic instability, Gaddafi positioned himself as the leader of a Pan-Arab and Pan-African movement, using state terror, media control, and oil wealth to consolidate his grip on power. His *Green Book* sought to create an ideological justification for his personal rule, much like Hitler's *Mein Kampf* or Mao's *Little Red Book*.

Mobutu and the Rhetoric of National Renewal – In the Congo (later named Zaire), Mobutu Sese Seko took control after a Western-backed coup against Prime Minister Patrice Lumumba. His authoritarian rule, from 1965 to 1997, was marked by extreme cronyism, militarized nationalism, and a cult of personality. Mobutu eliminated political rivals, enriched himself through state resources, and rebranded Zaire with his vision of "authenticity," banning Western clothing and renaming cities to reflect his nationalistic ideology.

Erdoğan and the Manufactured Crisis of Democracy – Recep Tayyip Erdoğan in Turkey has increasingly employed strongman tactics, exploiting the 2016 failed coup attempt to justify purges of political opponents, media suppression, and judicial overhauls. By manipulating Turkish nationalism and Islamism, he has centralized power, dismantled secular democratic institutions, and branded himself as the protector of Turkey against both Western and domestic "threats."

Orbán and the "Illiberal Christian Democracy" in Hungary – Viktor Orbán, Hungary's prime minister, has steadily eroded democracy since returning to power in 2010. Citing migration crises and national security threats, he has undermined judicial independence, taken control of media outlets, and passed laws to weaken opposition parties, promoting what he calls "illiberal Christian democracy."

Duterte and the War on Drugs in the Philippines – Rodrigo Duterte ascended to power by capitalizing on public fears about crime and drug-related violence. His brutal war on drugs, marked by extrajudicial killings and state-sponsored vigilantism, mirrored fascist strategies of using violence as a political tool. Duterte presented himself as an uncompromising leader willing to bypass legal institutions in the name of national security, echoing the rhetoric of past authoritarian rulers. His administration systematically eroded democratic institutions, intimidated journalists, and silenced critics, all while maintaining mass popularity through xenophobic nationalism and propaganda-driven media campaigns.

Bolsonaro and the Militarization of Brazilian Politics – Jair Bolsonaro (also called "Trump of the Tropics") leveraged political instability, economic recession, and anti-leftist sentiment to rise to power. Presenting himself as the savior of Brazil from corruption and socialist influence, Bolsonaro normalized political violence, attacked democratic institutions, and promoted deep social divisions. His administration's rhetoric frequently demonized marginalized communities, vilified Indigenous populations, LGBTQ+ individuals, and political opponents, and encouraged military nostalgia, mirroring the fascist glorification of past authoritarian regimes. Like other modern strongmen, he weaponized misinformation and social media to manipulate public opinion, using platforms like WhatsApp and Telegram to spread false narratives and conspiracy theories.

Putin and the Post-Soviet Crisis – Vladimir Putin emerged as Russia's dominant leader in the aftermath of the Soviet Union's collapse, during a period of economic instability, rising crime, and political disillusionment. Following the 1999 apartment bombings, which the government blamed on Chechen terrorists, Putin launched the Second Chechen War, using national security and law-and-order rhetoric to solidify his position. Over the years, he has dismantled democratic institutions, silenced dissent, and cultivated a personality cult, adapting traditional authoritarian strategies to modern Russia.

Trump and the Weaponization of Populist Rage – Donald Trump exploited economic anxieties, racial tensions, and political polarization to undermine democratic norms. Like fascist leaders before him, he vilified the press, scapegoated minorities, and promoted a cult of leadership, claiming "Nobody knows the system better than me, which is why I alone can fix it" (Marcus, 2018). The January 6, 2021, insurrection where he incited supporters to challenge the democratic transfer of power illustrated the real danger of authoritarian tendencies even within democratic nations.

These examples, among other fascist-leaning leaders, illustrate that authoritarianism remains a persistent threat, continuously adapting to contemporary political, economic, and social crises. Though their ideologies and tactics may vary, their strategies for consolidating power follow a familiar historical pattern, underscoring the need for constant vigilance in defending democracy.

Fascist Dynamics in the 21st Century

While today's strongmen may not always openly identify as fascists, they draw heavily from historically fascist playbooks, adapting their strategies to modern political and economic contexts. As Federico Finchelstein (2024) highlights in *The Wannabe Fascists: A Guide to Understanding the Greatest Threat to Democracy*, contemporary authoritarian leaders may stop short of establishing full dictatorships, yet they rely on xenophobia, propaganda, and political violence—three foundational pillars of fascism—to consolidate power while maintaining a facade of democratic legitimacy. Other studies, such as Jason Stanley's *How Fascism Works: The Politics of Us and Them* (2018) and *Erasing History: How Fascists Rewrite the Past to Control the Future* (2024), identify additional core dynamics of fascist strategies that have evolved and adapted but remain central to contemporary authoritarian practices.

Dynamic #1 - Economic Manipulations: Historically, fascist regimes relied on corporate elites and industrialists who saw economic opportunity in aligning with authoritarianism. Mussolini's Italy pioneered the "corporate state," merging state control with private industry while repressing labor movements to ensure economic stability. Hitler's Nazi Germany, similarly, secured the loyalty of business elites such as Krupp, I.G. Farben, and Siemens by promising profits in exchange for political allegiance, war production, and complicity in the regime's crimes. Today's strongmen continue this tradition of economic manipulation but in more sophisticated ways. Putin's Russia operates as a kleptocracy, where oligarchs retain their wealth and privilege in exchange for unwavering political loyalty. Erdoğan in Türkiye has funneled state resources to pro-government businesses, crushing independent economic entities that could challenge his rule. In the United States, Trump's economic policies—including deregulation, tax cuts for the wealthy, and the weakening of financial oversight—reinforced a system where business elites benefit from his administration, creating a financial stake in sustaining his leadership.

Dynamic #2 - Propaganda and Disinformation: Mussolini and Hitler tightly controlled the press, using state-run newspapers, radio broadcasts, and film to shape public perception. Mussolini's Ministry of Popular Culture ensured that only state-approved narratives were disseminated, while Nazi Germany's Joseph Goebbels orchestrated a propaganda machine that weaponized lies, staged events, and exploited mass psychology. They framed themselves as protectors of national identity while dehumanizing political opponents and minorities. Modern authoritarians have adapted these tactics to the digital age. Unlike total state control over the media, leaders like Trump, Putin, and Bolsonaro rely on fragmented yet influential media ecosystems—such as Fox News, state-sponsored Russian TV, and WhatsApp-driven misinformation in Brazil—to amplify their narratives while discrediting independent journalism. Putin employs online troll farms to flood social media with pro-Kremlin disinformation, while Trump's embrace of far-right media and conspiracy theories undermined trust in democratic institutions, particularly regarding elections. The strategic use of digital platforms allows authoritarian figures to manipulate public opinion without needing direct state ownership of the media.

Dynamic #3 - Pseudo-Democratic Legitimacy: Hitler and Mussolini initially rose to power through democratic means before dismantling democratic institutions entirely. Hitler used the Reichstag Fire in 1933 as a pretext to suspend civil liberties and arrest opposition leaders, paving the way for totalitarian rule. Mussolini manipulated Italy's political system by intimidating rivals and securing laws that granted him unchecked authority. Today's authoritarians rarely abolish elections outright but instead, hollow out democracy from within. Putin holds elections where opposition candidates are jailed or assassinated, maintaining a veneer of legitimacy. Erdoğan, Orbán, and Modi manipulate electoral laws, judicial independence, and media access to ensure their continued rule while still holding elections as a formality. Trump's efforts to overturn the 2020 U.S. election—culminating in the January 6th insurrection—demonstrate how modern authoritarians attempt to subvert democracy through legal maneuvers, propaganda, and direct incitement rather than outright abolition.

Dynamic #4 - Xenophobia, Scapegoating, and Division: A core strategy of historical fascism was the creation of an "enemy within" to unify followers. Nazi Germany scapegoated Jews, communists, and other marginalized groups as existential threats, justifying their persecution. Mussolini's Italy vilified socialists, intellectuals, and Slavic minorities, promoting a hyper-nationalist vision of Italian supremacy. Contemporary strongmen employ similar tactics but with updated targets. Trump framed immigrants, Muslims, and journalists as national threats, branding his movement with the exclusionary "America First" doctrine. Orbán in Hungary has built his political identity on anti-migrant rhetoric, while Bolsonaro and Modi have targeted LGBTQ+ communities, Indigenous groups, and religious minorities. This manufactured "us-versus-them" dynamic fosters loyalty among supporters while justifying authoritarian policies.

Dynamic #5 - Political Violence and Intimidation: Mussolini's Blackshirts *(Camice Nere,* officially called *Milizia Volontaria per la Sicurezza Nazionale, MVSN)* and Hitler's SA *(Stormtroopers)* were paramilitary forces that terrorized opposition figures, violently suppressing dissent. These squads operated with state approval, using intimidation and outright assassination to eliminate political threats. While modern authoritarians rarely deploy official paramilitary units, they instead encourage or tolerate political violence from extremist supporters. Putin's regime has assassinated critics and used secret police tactics to maintain fear. Trump emboldened far-right militia groups, culminating in the January 6th

Capitol attack and then pardoning all of them when he returned to office. Duterte in the Philippines promoted extrajudicial killings under the guise of a drug war, targeting political enemies and the poor. The shift from state-run paramilitaries to unofficial yet state-endorsed violence reflects an adaptation of historical fascist tactics to contemporary legal and political realities.

Dynamic #6 - Anti-Intellectualism and the Attack on Critical Education: Fascist regimes have historically waged war against intellectuals, academics, and educators. The Nazis burned books, expelled Jewish and leftist professors, and replaced objective scholarship with state-approved ideology. Mussolini sought to reshape Italian education to glorify the state and discourage critical thinking. Modern authoritarian leaders continue this tradition by attacking critical education, branding it as subversive. For example, Trump and right-wing politicians in the U.S. have pushed for book bans, restricted discussions on race and gender, defunded higher education, and even proposed drastic measures like signing an executive order to eliminate the Department of Education. Orbán's Hungary has dismantled gender studies programs and undermined academic freedom, while Bolsonaro sought to defund public universities. By weakening education systems, today's authoritarians create a more malleable populace that is less likely to resist their targeted propaganda.

Dynamic #7 - Dehumanization and the Erosion of Empathy: Fascist regimes relied on dehumanization to justify atrocities, portraying Jews, Slavs, and political dissidents as subhuman threats. Nazi propaganda depicted Jewish people as rats and communists as disease-ridden enemies, facilitating mass persecution. Today's authoritarian leaders employ similar tactics to justify harsh policies. Trump described migrants as "animals" and "invaders," rationalizing family separation at the border. Modi's government in India has encouraged violent rhetoric against Muslims, while Bolsonaro dismissed the deaths of Indigenous and impoverished communities from COVID-19 as inevitable. By stripping people of their humanity, these leaders erode societal empathy, enabling policies that violate human rights.

Dynamic #8 - Conspiracy Theories and Simplistic Solutions: Nazi Germany thrived on conspiratorial thinking, from blaming Jews for economic woes to fabricating threats of communist uprisings. Mussolini similarly painted all opposition as foreign-controlled saboteurs. Today's authoritarians rely on conspiracy theories to maintain control and distract from systemic failures. Trump fueled QAnon beliefs, promoted election fraud myths, and branded opposition as part of a "deep state" plot. Bolsonaro spread misinformation about vaccines and climate change, dismissing scientific consensus as elite deception. Putin regularly frames opposition movements as foreign conspiracies. These tactics not only consolidate power but also create an alternate reality where authoritarian leaders become the sole arbiters of truth.

Though the tools and technologies have evolved, modern authoritarian leaders continue to employ fascist-era strategies to consolidate power, erode democratic norms, and manipulate public sentiment. Recognizing these patterns is crucial to resisting authoritarian creep and defending democratic values in an era where history's darkest lessons remain alarmingly relevant. While these dynamics vary across different geographical and cultural contexts, they exhibit strikingly similar characteristics to historical Nazi-Fascist regimes. As Finchelstein warns, today's "wannabe fascists" may not yet be full dictators, but they are systematically dismantling democracy by exploiting crises, manufacturing enemies, and distorting public perception—steps that have historically paved the way for full-fledged fascist rule. By studying how past fascist regimes rose to power—and how today's leaders mirror their strategies—we can recognize the warning signs early and take action to prevent authoritarianism from fully taking hold.

Fascist Leadership: The Cult of the Strongman

Fascist regimes thrive on the myth of the infallible leader—a figure who embodies the nation, commands absolute loyalty, and demands obedience under the guise of strength. These leaders cultivate an image of decisive action, portraying themselves as the only solution to national decline or external threats. The cult of the strongman is built through propaganda, spectacle, and the systematic dismantling of democratic checks and balances. By stoking fears of instability and offering authoritarian control as the antidote, fascist leaders consolidate power, silencing opposition and eliminating perceived enemies. To understand fascist leadership dynamics, one needs to understand how the cult of personality, a hallmark of fascist leadership, from Mussolini and Hitler to modern autocrats, and how their rhetoric and tactics resonate across generations.

In *Strongmen: Mussolini to the Present,* Ruth Ben-Ghiat (2020) traces the evolution of authoritarian leadership and the enduring strategies of strongmen in consolidating power. A central theme in her analysis is the cult of personality, a tactic perfected by Benito Mussolini and echoed in modern leaders like Vladimir Putin, Silvio Berlusconi, and Donald Trump. The cult of the strongman relies on hyper-masculinity, media manipulation, and the fusion of political power with personal branding.

Mussolini, a former journalist, was a master of self-mythologization, carefully curating his public image to project strength, vitality, and omnipotence. He staged elaborate spectacles, showcasing his physical prowess through activities like fencing, bare-chested agricultural work, and even posing as a modern-day Caesar. His image was ubiquitous, appearing on posters, coins, and schoolbooks, reinforcing his presence in everyday Italian life. Mussolini's fascist propaganda machine ensured that he was perceived not merely as a politician but as the embodiment of the Italian state. Ben-Ghiat demonstrates that this tradition of leader-centered propaganda did not disappear with fascism but evolved with modern media and consumer culture. She notes that "the cults that rose up around Mussolini and Hitler in the early 1920s answered anxieties about the decline of male status, the waning of traditional religious authority, and the loss of moral clarity" (p. 18).

In her analysis of Putin, she writes, "Putin's personality cult, anchored in his display of virility, melds Soviet-style sternness and patriotism with homages to post-Communist capitalist accumulation. His face can be found on myriad consumer items, with a price point for everyone, from special-edition gold Apple Watches, to bedding, T-shirts, and pottery" (Ben-Ghiat, 2020, p. 81). Like Mussolini, Putin meticulously cultivates a myth of invincibility, reinforcing his image as a decisive and formidable leader. His staged displays of strength—riding horses shirtless, practicing judo, and projecting a steely, authoritarian demeanor—mirror Mussolini's own carefully orchestrated spectacles of power. However, Putin modernizes the cult of personality, blending Soviet nostalgia with capitalist branding, ensuring his likeness is not only a political symbol but also a widely marketed commodity in Russia.

Silvio Berlusconi, while not a dictator, maintained a close personal and political alliance with Putin (Ben-Ghiat, 2020, Introduction). He borrowed heavily from Mussolini's media dominance strategy, taking advantage of his near-total control over Italy's television networks to shape public perception and reinforce his populist appeal. His personal brand—crafted around the image of a charismatic, self-made billionaire and Milan soccer team owner—positioned himself as Italy's savior from political incompetence. This narrative strongly echoed Mussolini's own claims of being the sole leader capable of restoring order and national strength.

Donald Trump took this strategy even further, leveraging celebrity culture and reality television to manufacture a strongman persona. His rallies resembled entertainment events, filled with chants, slogans, and mass-produced merchandise designed to cultivate loyalty and identity. Like Mussolini, Trump positioned himself as the savior of the nation, someone who alone could "drain the swamp" and protect the country from perceived enemies.

The cult of the strongman remains a powerful force in contemporary politics, as today's authoritarian and charismatic leaders—despite ideological differences—continue to rely on similar strategies to consolidate power. Their leadership styles are defined by the following key characteristics:

1. **Hyper-Masculinity** – Strongmen project an image of physical and political dominance to reinforce their authority (Mussolini's military poses, Putin's shirtless displays, Trump's aggressive rhetoric).

2. **Narrative Control** – They manipulate television, newspapers, and social media to shape a narrative that elevates their status while silencing opposition (Berlusconi's media empire, Putin's state-controlled news, Trump's social media-based propaganda).

3. **Personal Branding** – Their image becomes a commodity, reinforcing their presence in both politics and popular culture (Mussolini's statues and posters, Putin's luxury-branded merchandise, Trump's red MAGA hats and reality-TV persona).

4. **Messianic Leadership** – They position themselves as the sole saviors of their nations, claiming to be the only ones capable of restoring order and greatness (Mussolini's fascist vision, Putin's nationalist revival, Trump's "only I can fix it" mentality).

By analyzing Mussolini's legacy, Ben-Ghiat illustrates how modern strongmen—including Hitler, Franco, Gaddafi, Pinochet, Mobutu, Gaddafi, Putin, Berlusconi, and Trump—adapt and refine the cult of personality for contemporary audiences, demonstrating that authoritarian tendencies persist even within democratic systems.

Fascism and the Manipulation of Information

Decades after Mussolini, Italy witnessed a similar fascination with another charismatic figure, Silvio Berlusconi, whose rise to political prominence (*La Discesa in Campo*, Naím, 2022) was significantly driven by his control of mass media. Berlusconi utilized television and media ownership to craft a compelling, populist narrative, appealing directly to Italians who were disillusioned by political stagnation, economic uncertainty, and widespread corruption scandals. Much like Mussolini before him, Berlusconi projected an image of decisive leadership and national renewal, promising prosperity and stability. His media empire allowed him to shape public opinion and redefine political discourse, capturing the imagination and trust of a populace longing for a figure capable of restoring Italy's international stature and domestic confidence. As Orsina (2018) observes, Berlusconi's success was rooted in his ability to present himself as a businessman outsider, crafting a political style that fused entertainment with governance. The parallels between Mussolini's authoritarian appeal and Berlusconi's populist charisma highlight a recurrent theme in Italian political history. A collective attraction to strong, charismatic leaders promising dramatic solutions in times of uncertainty.

Examining Mussolini, Berlusconi, and Trump reveals notable similarities in their leadership styles, particularly their reliance on charismatic authority, media influence, and populist rhetoric. Each leader skillfully leveraged national anxieties, portraying themselves as outsiders challenging entrenched political elites and promising a restoration of lost national prestige. Mussolini harnessed print media and rallies, Berlusconi dominated television and media networks, and Trump mastered social media platforms bypassing traditional forms of television and newspapers. Their leadership styles prioritized personal loyalty, cultivated through powerful public personas and nationalist messages, often at the expense of democratic institutions and norms. Collectively, their political legacies demonstrate the potent combination of media-driven charisma and populist appeal and highlight the ongoing vulnerability of democracies to authoritarian impulses when societies seek simplistic answers to complex societal challenges. Modern populist and authoritarian leaders all master or control media communication, ensuring their messages dominate public discourse while marginalizing dissenting voices.

Table 4.2 provides a comparative analysis of key authoritarian leaders—Mussolini, Berlusconi, Trump, Orbán, Erdoğan, Modi, Xi, Putin, and Bukele—highlighting their leadership styles, media strategies, and overall impact on democratic institutions. A central theme across these leaders is their ability to manipulate information ecosystems to consolidate power, silence dissent, and shape public perception.

Through direct control over state-run media, co-opting private outlets, or weaponizing social media, these leaders have systematically undermined independent journalism and used disinformation as a political tool. Mussolini's regime perfected propaganda as a means of controlling national identity, while Putin and Xi have leveraged digital surveillance and censorship to maintain tight control over political narratives. Leaders like Trump, Berlusconi, and Bukele have capitalized on populist rhetoric and media spectacle, turning mass communication into a tool for personal branding and political legitimacy. Meanwhile, Orbán, Erdoğan, and Modi have implemented legal and economic pressures to suppress critical voices, eroding press freedom under the guise of national security and cultural preservation.

This sample of leaders' communication dynamics demonstrates that authoritarian leaders tend to follow a common playbook for media manipulation and public control. By monopolizing information channels, discrediting opposition voices, and cultivating echo chambers, these leaders exploit societal divisions and distort public discourse to serve their political interests.

A key element of their strategy is the deliberate use of conspiracy theories and "fake news" narratives to delegitimize critics, erode trust in independent institutions, and blur the line between fact and fiction (Finchelstein, 2022). By framing dissent as the product of shadowy elites, foreign adversaries, or internal subversives, they create an environment where objective truth is constantly in question. Leaders like Trump, Bolsonaro, and Orbán have weaponized accusations of "fake news" to discredit investigative journalism, while Putin and Xi have promoted state-backed disinformation to shape geopolitical narratives and suppress domestic unrest. Similarly, figures such as Erdoğan and Modi have leveraged nationalist conspiracies to justify crackdowns on opposition groups, portraying dissent as a threat to national security and cultural identity.

These tactics not only reinforce authoritarian control but also weaken democratic norms by fostering widespread cynicism and polarization. As misinformation becomes mainstream and fact-based discourse erodes, citizens struggle to critically engage with political realities, making it easier for authoritarian figures to entrench their power.

Table 4.2: Fascist Dynamics in Authoritarian Leaders

LEADER	FASCIST DYNAMICS (LEADERSHIP STYLE, MEDIA CONTROL, AND IMPACT ON DEMOCRACY)
BENITO MUSSOLINI (1922–1943)	Original fascist model; militaristic authoritarianism, propaganda through mass rallies and controlled media; abolished democratic institutions, implemented totalitarian governance.
SILVIO BERLUSCONI (1994–2011, NON-CONTINUOUSLY)	Populist authoritarian elements; personalized media empire and television dominance; weakened democratic institutions, promoted personality cult.
DONALD TRUMP (2017–2021; 2025–PRESENT)	Populist nationalism echoing fascist themes; direct communication via social media; challenged democratic norms, fostered polarization, undermined institutional trust.
VIKTOR ORBÁN (2010–PRESENT)	Illiberal authoritarian populism with fascist tendencies; state-controlled media, nationalist messaging; systematically weakened judicial independence, limited political freedoms.

RECEP TAYYIP ERDOĞAN (2003–PRESENT)	Authoritarian populism with fascist elements; centralized media control, religious nationalism; suppressed opposition, consolidated executive power, eroded democratic structures.
NARENDRA MODI (2014–PRESENT)	Populist strongman leadership aligning with fascist nationalism; sophisticated digital media strategy, Hindu nationalism; curtailed press freedoms, increased centralization of authority.
XI JINPING (2013–PRESENT)	Communist authoritarianism sharing fascist features; state propaganda, censorship, mass surveillance; abolished presidential term limits, reinforced single-party totalitarian control.
VLADIMIR PUTIN (1999–PRESENT)	Nationalist authoritarianism resonating with fascist traits; extensive propaganda and media suppression; eliminated effective political opposition, entrenched long-term personal rule.
NAYIB BUKELE (2019–PRESENT)	Authoritarian populism with fascistic elements; aggressive social media strategy, state propaganda emphasizing security threats; centralized power, suspended constitutional rights, implemented mass incarceration ("mega prison" policy), and weakened democratic checks and balances.

By analyzing these figures, we can see how media-driven populism, combined with nationalist rhetoric and personal branding, has shaped political landscapes across different historical periods. The works of Eatwell (2017) and Mounk (2018) further explore how contemporary populism mirrors past authoritarian tendencies, reinforcing the need to safeguard democratic resilience against the allure of strongman leadership.

Understanding Fascism as a Mindset

Fascism is often dismissed as a historical aberration—something confined to the darkest chapters of the 20th century, exemplified by Nazi Germany, Mussolini's Italy, and Franco's Spain. In doing so, we risk misunderstanding its true nature. Fascism is not merely a political regime; it is a mindset—one that feeds on fear, thrives in polarization, and slowly corrodes democratic institutions from within. Much like normalcy bias, the cognitive distortion that leads people to underestimate the possibility or impact of a disaster, societies often believe, *"It could never happen here."* They view fascism as a catastrophic train wreck: horrifying to witness, yet always someone else's tragedy.

But fascism does not arrive fully formed. It grows incrementally, tolerated in small doses—through voter suppression, media manipulation, and attacks on dissent—until it metastasizes into something far more dangerous. In this way, fascism is more like cancer than catastrophe: silent, mutating over time, adapting to its host, and only becoming visible when the damage is already extensive. Like metastatic cancer, it disregards boundaries, invades neighboring territories, and ultimately destroys its host in a selfish pursuit of power. And just as cancer treatment often involves collateral damage—seen metaphorically in actions like the atomic bombing of Hiroshima and Nagasaki—societies sometimes inflict harm on the innocent in their desperation to root out authoritarianism. Yet, as with modern medicine, early detection and targeted response offer hope. Understanding fascism not just as a historical phenomenon but as a recurring mindset is the first step in developing the civic "immune system" necessary to detect and resist its return.

Most importantly, fascism is not sustained by leaders alone—it is legitimized by followers who, especially in times of crisis or uncertainty, are drawn to displays of strength and promises of order. Authoritarian leaders often mask fascist tendencies beneath the allure of charisma, decisiveness, and national pride. This makes recognition more difficult, as the desire for stability or bold leadership can overshadow early warning signs of repression. The cult of the strongman thrives when people project their hopes onto seemingly confident figures who claim to offer simple solutions to complex problems. As a result, rhetoric that undermines democratic norms becomes normalized, and authoritarian tactics are excused or even embraced. This is why fascism must be understood not only as a system of government but as a mindset—a worldview that glorifies power, suppresses dissent, and redefines loyalty as submission. While its outward forms may shift with cultural or technological change, its core logic remains the same. Recognizing fascism as a recurring pattern of behavior and belief is essential to identifying its presence in contemporary society and resisting its slow, often seductive advance.

In other words, understanding fascism requires more than identifying historical regimes; it demands recognition of the underlying mindset that fuels authoritarianism, exclusion, and control. As originally analyzed by Trotsky in the 1930s (reprinted in 2002) and later developed by contemporary authors like Stanley (2018) and Tiburi (2021), fascist worldviews are deeply intertwined with cultural patterns of machismo, nationalism, and xenophobia—psychosocial forces that normalize dominance, suppress dialogue, and marginalize perceived outsiders. This mindset upholds rigid hierarchies and thrives on fear and division, shaping behaviors across political, social, and personal domains. While no single ideology stands as fascism's perfect inverse, contrasting worldviews—such as liberal democracy, democratic socialism, and anarchism—challenge its core tenets by advocating for decentralized power, civil liberties, and pluralistic inclusion. The political spectrum is nuanced, but any framework that fundamentally opposes authoritarian control, supremacist thinking, and the erosion of individual rights aligns with an anti-fascist ethic. By understanding these opposing values, we can more clearly identify how fascist tendencies manifest across institutions—from politics and education to religion and culture—and how resistance is rooted not only in systems, but in the everyday defense of democracy, diversity, and human dignity.

The fascist mindset is fundamentally rooted in hierarchical power, the glorification of strength, and the suppression of dissent. It operates through divisive narratives that frame society in rigid us vs. them terms, privileging the dominant group while justifying the oppression of others. In politics, it demands blind obedience to a singular authority; in national identity, it fuels exclusionary nationalism that views diversity as a threat; and in economics, it prioritizes corporate-state alliances that enrich elites while exploiting workers. Truth is manipulated, history rewritten, and education censored to reinforce the regime's ideology. Fear and violence—whether through state repression, propaganda, or intimidation—are used to maintain control. Even religion is co-opted, framing opposition as heretical and aligning faith with the state's goals (Pollard, 2011).

While its expression may shift across historical and cultural contexts, the fascist mindset follows a recognizable pattern—from Nazi Germany's militarized nationalism to Mussolini's corporatism and Franco's religious authoritarianism. Though contemporary versions may not always label themselves as fascist, they adapt these historical models to modern political, economic, and technological realities. Recognizing and resisting this mindset is essential in safeguarding democratic institutions, civil liberties, and a just society. Table 4.3 presents a comparative analysis of fascist and anti-fascist mindsets, highlighting their contrasting values and leadership outcomes. This overview provides valuable insights into the ideological differences and their broader implications.

Table 4.3: Fascist and Anti-Fascist Mindsets

Field	Fascist Mindset	Anti-Fascist Mindset
Politics	Authoritarian rule, centralized power, suppression of dissent, cult of personality.	Democratic governance, accountability, participatory decision-making, protection of civil liberties.

ECONOMICS	State-corporate alliances, economic inequality, suppression of labor rights, exploitation for national strength.	Economic equity, labor protections, fair markets, prioritization of social well-being.
EDUCATION	Indoctrination, censorship, historical revisionism, suppression of critical thinking.	Education for critical thinking, historical accuracy, intellectual freedom, open discourse.
PSYCHOLOGY	Fear-based obedience, dehumanization of opponents, creation of scapegoats.	Empathy, psychological resilience, rejection of fear-based manipulation, fostering inclusion.
MEDIA & INFORMATION	Propaganda, misinformation, suppression of independent journalism, control over public discourse.	Media literacy, transparency, support for independent journalism, combating misinformation.
RELIGION	Co-opting religion for political control, portraying dissent as heresy, weaponizing faith.	Separation of religion and state, ethical integrity, protection of religious freedom.
SOCIAL IDENTITY	Exclusive nationalism, racial and ethnic hierarchies, 'us vs. them' mentality.	Pluralism, multiculturalism, solidarity, human rights-based social policies.
LAW & JUSTICE	Politicization of justice, erosion of judicial independence, laws serving the regime.	Independent judiciary, equal justice under law, protection of civil rights.

CRISIS MANAGEMENT	Exploitation of crises to justify authoritarian measures, blaming external/internal enemies.	Crisis mitigation through democratic processes, addressing root causes, global cooperation.
INTERNATIONAL RELATIONS	Militarization, imperialist aggression, rejection of international cooperation, nationalism over global stability.	Diplomatic engagement, multilateralism, promotion of peace and human rights.
TECHNOLOGY & SURVEILLANCE	Use of mass surveillance, data manipulation, AI-driven authoritarian control, censorship, and suppression of digital dissent.	Protection of digital privacy, ethical AI governance, transparency, open-source technology, and freedom of online expression.
PUBLIC HEALTH & SCIENCE	Politicization of science, suppression of medical dissent, anti-intellectualism, and use of health crises to justify authoritarian control.	Evidence-based policymaking, accessibility of healthcare for all, promotion of scientific literacy, and protection of medical ethics.
CULTURE & ARTS	Censorship of artistic expression, state-controlled propaganda in cultural production, suppression of diverse perspectives.	Freedom of artistic expression, funding for diverse cultural narratives, and the role of art as a tool for critical thought and social justice.
GENDER & FAMILY POLICY	Enforcement of rigid gender roles, suppression of LGBTQ+ rights, promotion of a	Gender equity, protection of LGBTQ+ rights, and policies that support diverse family structures and personal freedoms.

	patriarchal, state-defined family structure.	
ENVIRONMENTAL POLICY & SUSTAINABILITY	Exploitation of natural resources for nationalist expansion, denial of climate science, suppression of environmental activism.	Commitment to climate justice, sustainability, and policies that protect ecosystems and marginalized communities.
LABOR & WORKFORCE RIGHTS	Corporatist alliances that benefit elites, suppression of labor unions, worker exploitation as a patriotic duty.	Workers' rights, fair wages, union protections, and an economy that prioritizes human dignity over corporate profit.
HISTORY & MEMORY	Revisionist history, erasure of atrocities, glorification of authoritarian figures, suppression of critical historical inquiry.	Historical accuracy, acknowledgment of past injustices, public memory preservation, and promotion of truth in education.
URBAN PLANNING & PUBLIC SPACE	Monuments and architecture used to glorify the state, exclusion of marginalized communities from public space, militarization of urban areas.	Inclusive urban planning, public spaces designed for democratic participation, memorialization of resistance movements.
JUSTICE & POLICING	Militarized policing, mass incarceration, law enforcement used as a tool of state repression.	Community-based justice, accountability in law enforcement, legal protections for marginalized groups.

PHILOSOPHY & ETHICS	Moral absolutism, rejection of pluralism, obedience to authority over ethical reasoning.	Ethical inquiry, philosophical diversity, moral reasoning based on justice and human dignity.

Understanding mindsets is not about influencing how one thinks or imposing a specific worldview—it is about fostering conscious awareness and ensuring that opinions and beliefs are formed independently, free from manipulation and coercion. A democratic society respects diverse perspectives, but informed thinking requires critical discernment—the ability to recognize when ideas are being shaped by fear, propaganda, or deliberate distortion. The goal of analyzing fascist and anti-fascist mindsets is not to dictate thought but to provide tools for reflection, ensuring that individuals engage with history, politics, and society with awareness rather than indoctrination.

Understanding the fascist mindset is not just an academic exercise—it is essential to protecting the principles that define a just and democratic society. Authoritarian tendencies do not always emerge through overt force; they take root through gradual normalization, often disguised as patriotism, economic revival, or a return to traditional values. These forces manipulate grievances and fears, distorting ideals like freedom, security, and national identity to justify exclusion, hierarchy, and repression. Recognizing these patterns allows us to resist the erosion of civil liberties, the manipulation of truth, and the creeping acceptance of oppression.

At the same time, understanding the anti-fascist mindset underscores the values of democratic accountability, human dignity, and social solidarity—principles that serve as a foundation for a more just and resilient society. But resisting authoritarianism requires more than political opposition; it demands active discernment, a conscious effort to define where our values truly lie and to commit ourselves to a vision of the future grounded in inclusivity, justice, and collective well-being. Do we choose solidarity over division, truth over manipulation, and dignity over dehumanization? The fate of any society is not predetermined—it is shaped by the choices we make, the values we defend, and the principles we refuse to compromise. By cultivating critical awareness through education, civic engagement, and ethical reflection, we ensure that democracy is not merely preserved, but strengthened, guiding us toward a future of greater equity, resilience, and shared humanity.

Fascist Leadership as Concentration of Power

Fascist and authoritarian dynamics are not merely a mindset; they are deliberate strategies designed to centralize power. These systems rely on calculated actions to dismantle opposition and weaken accountability mechanisms, ensuring absolute control. No matter their different typologies, they are leadership practices characterized by the concentration of power in the hands of a single leader or a small ruling elite, effectively dismantling democratic institutions and civil liberties. The historical examples of Nazi Germany under Adolf Hitler and Fascist Italy under Benito Mussolini demonstrate how consolidating executive, legislative, and judicial authority leads to unchecked governmental control, repression, and human rights violations. Similar patterns of concentrated power have been observed in later authoritarian regimes, including Augusto Pinochet's dictatorship in Chile, Francisco Franco's Spain, and modern examples such as Vladimir Putin's Russia.

In Nazi Germany, Adolf Hitler capitalized on the weaknesses of the Weimar Republic and the Reichstag Fire Decree of 1933 to justify the suppression of political opposition. The passage of the Enabling Act that same year granted Hitler legislative authority, effectively nullifying parliamentary democracy. As Ian Kershaw (1998) notes, "Hitler's power rested on a legal revolution, destroying democracy from within its own framework" (p. 456). The judiciary, too, became an instrument of Nazi ideology, rendering courts complicit in the regime's authoritarian rule.

Similarly, Benito Mussolini eroded democratic structures in Italy by centralizing authority under his leadership. Through the 1925–1926 Fascist Laws, Mussolini eliminated political opposition and dismantled independent institutions. Historian R.J.B. Bosworth (2006) describes Mussolini's approach, "He transformed Italy into a personalist dictatorship where power radiated from his singular authority, crushing dissent and rendering political pluralism obsolete" (p. 312).

Beyond Europe, Augusto Pinochet's 1973 coup in Chile established a military dictatorship that concentrated power through repression and the suppression of democratic governance. The Chilean judiciary remained largely ineffective in countering human rights abuses, a hallmark of authoritarian consolidation. Steve Stern (2004) observes, "The junta systematically undermined democratic norms, replacing them with a regime of fear and absolute executive control" (p. 176).

The fundamental safeguard against authoritarian overreach is the independence of the executive, legislative, and judicial branches. Montesquieu's theory of separation of powers emphasizes that "there is no liberty if the judiciary power be not separated from the legislative and executive" (1748, p. 81). The collapse of these divisions facilitates the rise of authoritarianism, even within well-established democracies.

In the United States, the risk of power centralization has surfaced in moments of crisis. Richard Nixon's Watergate scandal and Donald Trump's attempts to challenge the 2020 election results illustrate the importance of robust institutional checks. James Madison warned in *The Federalist Papers*, "The accumulation of all powers, legislative, executive, and judiciary, in the same hands... may justly be pronounced the very definition of tyranny" (Federalist No. 47).

The American Fascist Paradox

While American democratic institutions have demonstrated remarkable resilience, they remain vulnerable to erosion. Threats such as court-packing, executive overreach, and legislative dysfunction weaken the system of checks and balances. However, institutional safeguards alone are insufficient to defend democracy. A free and critical press, robust political opposition, and engaged civil society are essential counterweights to authoritarian tendencies. Investigative journalism exposes corruption, opposition parties prevent unchecked power, and mass movements exert direct pressure on leaders to uphold democratic principles. Without civic vigilance, democracy risks succumbing to power centralization—the defining feature of authoritarian rule.

Ironically, the United States played a decisive role in defeating fascism during World War II, yet fascist tendencies have long been embedded within its own political and cultural fabric. Kagan (2024) argues in *Rebellion: How Antiliberalism Is Tearing America Apart—Again*, the same rebellious spirit that fueled the American Revolution has also nurtured deep strains of antiliberalism, anti-intellectualism, and hostility toward government regulation. What began as resistance to monarchy and centralized control evolved, in certain factions, into a rejection of pluralism, expertise, and democratic institutions. This paradox—where "freedom" is invoked to justify exclusion, authoritarianism, and state-backed corporate power—has allowed fascist-adjacent ideologies to take root, particularly in moments of economic and social crisis. Steinmetz-Jenkins (2024), in *Did It Happen Here? Perspectives on Fascism and America*, explores how these tendencies, often disguised under patriotic or populist rhetoric, resurface whenever historical memory fades and democratic safeguards weaken.

As Maddow (2023) documents in *Prequel: An American Fight Against Fascism*, even in the 1930s and 1940s—when the U.S. actively fought fascism abroad—domestic pro-fascist movements gained significant traction, attracting segments of the population sympathetic to authoritarianism. With the passing of the generation that directly confronted fascism, these ideological currents have resurfaced, amplified by disinformation, cultural polarization, and attacks on historical awareness. Today, economic grievances and social anxieties are manipulated to normalize authoritarian policies, creating an environment where democratic backsliding is framed as patriotic necessity.

Nowhere is this paradox more evident than in the ideology of American exceptionalism. Blau (2017) critiques this contradiction, noting that while the U.S. positions itself as a champion of democracy and human rights, it frequently resists international accountability and multilateral cooperation. This selective application of liberal principles fosters a sense of impunity, allowing authoritarian tendencies to flourish under the guise of national sovereignty. Zürn (2024) expands on this idea, arguing that the contested nature of the American liberal script has fueled a uniquely powerful authoritarian populist movement. Unlike other democracies where populism remains at the margins, Trumpism commands support from nearly half the electorate, illustrating how American exceptionalism paradoxically weakens its own democratic institutions.

The contradictions within American liberalism echo de Tocqueville's warning about the "tyranny of the majority" (Tocqueville 1994 [1835/1840], Part 2, Ch. 7, 8). Börze et al. (2024) highlight fundamental tensions in American political culture—between majority rule and minority rights, capitalism and social solidarity, national identity and cosmopolitanism. These contradictions provide fertile ground for leaders who exploit grievances to consolidate power. The resurgence of fascist tendencies in the U.S. is not merely a historical recurrence but an embedded feature of its political culture, where the very ideology of exceptionalism creates the conditions for democratic crisis.

This paradox is further illustrated by America's treatment of immigration. Despite being a nation built by immigrants, the U.S. has a long history of xenophobia, from the Chinese Exclusion Act to the internment of Japanese Americans and recent border policies. This extends to other marginalized groups. As Gessen (2025) highlights, Trump-era policies targeting transgender individuals were not simply acts of discrimination but deliberate attempts at "denationalization"— the stripping away of legal and social recognition. Such tactics align with broader fascist strategies that seek to construct an exclusionary national identity by scapegoating vulnerable populations.

Another glaring contradiction lies in the U.S. commitment to Jewish rights after the Holocaust while simultaneously failing to address ongoing human rights violations against other marginalized groups, including immigrants, racial minorities, and LGBTQ+ individuals. This selective application of human rights principles weakens their legitimacy, revealing a pattern where the defense of justice is contingent on political convenience rather than universal moral obligation.

Pastor Martin Niemöller's famous warning, "First they came for the Socialists, and I did not speak out—because I was not a Socialist..." carries even more weight when we remember that he initially supported aspects of Nazism before becoming one of its most vocal critics. His transformation underscores the importance of moral awakening and the courage to speak out against injustice, even when it feels late. In a modern context, the sequence might read:

> First, they came for the undocumented immigrants, and I did not speak out because I was not an immigrant.
> Then they came for the transgender community, and I did not speak out because I was not transgender.
> Then they came for disabled people, and I did not speak out because I was not disabled.
> Then they came for the journalists, and I did not speak out because I was not a journalist.
> Then they came for the scientists, and I did not speak out because I was not a scientist.
> Then they came for the protestors, and I did not speak out because I was not protesting.
> Then they came for me, and there was no one left to speak for me.

This adapted warning highlights how the erosion of rights for any one group signals a broader assault on democracy itself. Historically, authoritarian regimes have targeted the most vulnerable first, using legal, social, and political mechanisms to normalize repression before expanding it to the broader population. Today, the same playbook is being used—through voter suppression, book bans, attacks on academic freedom, and the criminalization of dissent—under the guise of patriotism or national security.

Recognizing fascism as an enduring mindset, rather than a concluded historical chapter, is essential. The fight against authoritarianism is not an abstract ideological battle; it is a present-day struggle for truth, justice, and human dignity. Only through an anti-fascist consciousness—rooted in critical thinking, democratic values, and global solidarity—can we resist its resurgence and ensure that history's darkest lessons do not repeat themselves.

| 5 |

DECODING ANTI-FASCISM

"All ideas must be respected, except fascism. Fascism is not an idea; it is the death of all ideas."

— Sandro Pertini, former *Partigiano* and President of the Italian Republic

Anti-fascism, also spelled *antifascism*, refers to both a political ideology and a resistance movement that arose in the 1920s in direct response to the emergence of fascist regimes—most notably in Italy under Benito Mussolini and in Germany under Adolf Hitler. In this chapter, the hyphenated form *anti-fascism* is used deliberately to emphasize its broader, principled opposition to fascist ideas, policies, and practices. While *antifascism* (without the hyphen) often denotes a more formalized or ideological movement against authoritarianism, nationalism, and political oppression, *anti-fascism* highlights the everyday civic and moral stance against fascist tendencies wherever they appear. Closely linked to these traditions is the modern term "antifa", a shortened form of *antifascism*, rooted in early 20th-century European resistance movements such as Germany's *Antifaschistische Aktion*. Today, "antifa" is commonly associated with loosely organized activist groups confronting far-right extremism and defending democratic values (Bray, 2017). Taken together, anti-fascism, antifascism, and antifa represent a historical and ongoing commitment to protecting democracy, social justice, and human rights against the persistent threat of authoritarianism.

While it gained its most significant momentum during World War II, when the Axis powers were opposed not only by Allied governments but also by grassroots resistance movements worldwide, anti-fascism has continued in various forms to the present day. Unlike a singular ideology, anti-fascism has been embraced by diverse political traditions, including anarchism, communism, socialism, pacifism, republicanism, social democracy, and syndicalism, as well as centrist, liberal, conservative, and nationalist factions that opposed totalitarian rule. As a resistance movement, it was exemplified by underground fighters such as Josip Broz Tito in Yugoslavia and Jean Moulin of the French Resistance, who organized and led anti-Nazi efforts during World War II. In Italy, the partisan's resisters played a pivotal role in the fight against Nazi-Fascist occupation. Initially composed of former soldiers, the movement quickly grew to include various anti-fascist groups united in their struggle for liberation. Their efforts were instrumental in overthrowing fascist rule, and many of these resistance fighters later contributed to shaping Italy's post-war democratic government.

Antifascist leaders like Sandro Pertini and Ferruccio Parri embodied the shift from armed resistance to democratic governance in post-war Italy. Others, such as Enrico Berlinguer and Giorgio Napolitano, carried the values of the resistance into politics. Globally, figures like Churchill and Roosevelt led the fight against fascism, while thinkers like Antonio Gramsci and Hannah Arendt exposed its roots. Activists such as Dolores Ibárruri and Simone Weil bridged ideology and action. In later decades, leaders like Martin Luther King Jr. and Angela Davis extended the anti-fascist struggle to new forms of oppression. Whether through armed struggle, political leadership, or intellectual resistance, anti-fascism has remained a global force for democracy and justice. Table 5.1 highlights key anti-fascist figures whose courage, and sacrifice shaped this movement (Braskén et al., 2020).

Table 5.1: Anti-Fascist Leaders' Contributions

LEADER (CATEGORY, YEARS)	CONTRIBUTION (OPPOSITION AND LEGACY)
ANTONIO GRAMSCI, INTELLECTUAL - ITALY (1891-1937)	Developed the concept of cultural hegemony, resisted Mussolini; influential through the *Prison Notebooks* on ideology and power.
LUIGI ALBERTINI, INTELLECTUAL - ITALY (1871-1941)	Exposed Mussolini's abuses through journalism; challenged fascist propaganda as editor of *Corriere della Sera*.
GIOVANNI AMENDOLA, INTELLECTUAL - ITALY (1882-1926)	Led early opposition to Mussolini; became one of fascism's first martyrs after being attacked by fascist squads.
HANNAH ARENDT, INTELLECTUAL - GERMANY/USA (1906-1975)	Provided groundbreaking analysis of fascist totalitarianism, ideology, and terror in *The Origins of Totalitarianism*.
SIMONE WEIL, INTELLECTUAL - FRANCE (1909-1943)	Volunteered in Spanish Civil War against fascists; active in French Resistance; influential writings on oppression.
GEORGE ORWELL, INTELLECTUAL - UK (1903-1950)	Critiqued fascism and authoritarianism through literature; participated in Spanish Civil War; exposed totalitarian practices.
EMMA GOLDMAN, INTELLECTUAL - RUSSIA/USA (1869-1940)	Anarchist activist opposing fascism worldwide; advocated political freedoms, criticized dictatorship and militarism.
DIETRICH BONHOEFFER, RELIGIOUS LEADER - GERMANY (1906-1945)	Anti-Nazi theologian executed for opposing Hitler; promoted Christian ethics as basis for resistance.

DOROTHY DAY, RELIGIOUS LEADER - USA (1897-1980)	Opposed militarism and fascism; co-founded Catholic Worker Movement promoting peace, justice, care for the poor.
PIERRE-MARIE THÉAS, RELIGIOUS LEADER - FRANCE (1894-1977)	Publicly condemned Nazi persecution; resisted from captivity after Gestapo arrest.
OSCAR ROMERO, RELIGIOUS LEADER - EL SALVADOR (1917-1980)	Opposed state violence and militarism; assassinated during Mass, becoming a human rights symbol.
MAXIMILIAN KOLBE, RELIGIOUS LEADER – POLAND (1894-1941)	Opposed Nazi ideology, aided Jewish refugees; sacrificed his life at Auschwitz.
POPE PIUS XI, RELIGIOUS LEADER - VATICAN CITY (1857-1939)	Publicly condemned fascism and Nazi racism through encyclicals such as 'Mit Brennender Sorge'.
CARDINAL ALOYSIUS STEPINAC, RELIGIOUS LEADER - CROATIA (1898-1960)	Secretly aided Jews and dissidents under Nazi occupation; later opposed Communist repression.
WINSTON CHURCHILL, POLITICAL LEADER - UK (1874-1965)	Led Britain's resistance against Nazi Germany through speeches, diplomacy, military strategy.
FRANKLIN D. ROOSEVELT, POLITICAL LEADER - USA (1882-1945)	Mobilized the U.S. against global fascism; led wartime efforts and promoted democratic values.

JOSIP BROZ TITO, POLITICAL LEADER - YUGOSLAVIA (1892-1980)	Led Yugoslav Partisans against fascism; built effective guerrilla resistance in WWII.
SMEDLEY BUTLER, POLITICAL LEADER - USA (1881-1940)	Exposed fascist-backed coup attempt in the U.S.; prevented potential dictatorship through testimony.
HO CHI MINH, POLITICAL LEADER - VIETNAM (1890-1969)	Led Vietnamese resistance against Japanese fascism; advocated for national liberation from colonialism.
JEAN MOULIN, RESISTANCE FIGHTER - FRANCE (1899-1943)	Unified anti-Nazi factions in France; executed by Gestapo, becoming iconic martyr.
DOLORES IBÁRRURI, RESISTANCE FIGHTER - SPAIN (1895-1989)	Leader in Spanish Civil War; rallied Republicans against Franco's fascism with slogan 'No pasaran!'.
SANDRO PERTINI, RESISTANCE FIGHTER - ITALY (1896-1990)	Italian partisan; imprisoned by fascists; later influential post-war president shaping democratic Italy.
FERRUCCIO PARRI, RESISTANCE FIGHTER - ITALY (1890-1981)	Led Italian resistance; became first post-war Prime Minister, critical to liberation efforts.
VIRGILIA D'ANDREA, RESISTANCE FIGHTER - ITALY (1888-1933)	Anarchist poet exiled for anti-fascism; inspired anti-authoritarian movements.

WOODY GUTHRIE, ARTIST & CULTURAL FIGURE - USA (1912-1967)	Folk musician: combated fascism through music, famously stating 'This Machine Kills Fascists'.
PABLO PICASSO, ARTIST & CULTURAL FIGURE - SPAIN/FRANCE (1881-1973)	Created anti-fascist masterpiece 'Guernica', exposing horrors of fascism in the Spanish Civil War.
BERTOLT BRECHT, ARTIST & CULTURAL FIGURE - GERMANY (1898-1956)	Critiqued fascism through satirical plays; highlighted authoritarian dangers.
CHARLIE CHAPLIN, ARTIST & CULTURAL FIGURE - UK/USA (1889-1977)	Satirized fascism and Hitler through film, notably in The Great Dictator.
ALAN TURING, MATHEMATICIAN & SCIENTIST - UK (1912-1954)	Decoded Nazi communications; significantly contributed to Allied victory in WWII.
MARC CHAGALL, ARTIST & CULTURAL FIGURE - FRANCE/RUSSIA (1887-1985)	Created influential anti-fascist art; fled Nazi persecution, depicted resistance themes.

Many anti-fascist leaders played a crucial role in reconstructing societies after the devastation of Nazi-fascist regimes in Italy, Germany, and Japan, embedding democratic governance, social justice, and economic stability into their national frameworks. Their sacrifices and contributions helped enshrine fundamental rights in their countries' constitutions, ensuring that the horrors of fascism would not be repeated. For example, Sandro Pertini and Palmiro Togliatti helped write the Italian Constitution that prioritized universal healthcare, education, and workers' rights (Gilbert, 2024; Pugliese, 2004). In Germany, leaders such as Willy Brandt and Konrad Adenauer championed democratic renewal, embedding social market economics into the Basic Law (Grundgesetz), leading to the economic miracle (Wirtschaftswunder) and a strong welfare state (Agocs, 2017). In Japan, reformers like Shigeru Yoshida contributed to their constitution that promoted pacifism, democracy, and social welfare, leading to rapid post-war economic growth (Hein, 2018; Kersten, 2013). These leaders not only balanced political rights, social values, and economic prosperity but also helped their nations surpass older democracies in securing fundamental rights such as health, education, and housing, demonstrating that resilience, justice, and inclusive governance are essential for a flourishing society.

Anti-Fascism and Economic Justice

Anti-fascism is not only a political stance—it also entails the rejection of exclusionary, undemocratic economic systems that underpin authoritarian rule. Fascist regimes such as Nazi Germany and Mussolini's Italy pursued nationalist, autarkic economic models that deliberately prioritized state control and isolation over international cooperation. These economies emphasized centralized authority, subordinating markets and production to ideological goals, militarization, and rigid social hierarchies—at the expense of equity, labor rights, and inclusive development.

A core element of fascist economic strategy was the use of protectionist tariffs to shield domestic industries from foreign competition. Mussolini's Italy, for example, imposed high tariffs to promote national production and reduce dependency on imports, in line with his vision of economic self-sufficiency—or autarky. In the United States, the 1930 Smoot-Hawley Tariff Act (though not rooted in fascist ideology) followed a similar nationalistic rationale and contributed to a sharp decline in international trade, intensifying the global economic crisis of the Great Depression.

In Italy, when protectionist policies failed to deliver stability or prosperity, Mussolini redirected national frustration toward imperialist aggression—most notably the invasion of Ethiopia in 1935. These ventures resulted in heavy human and financial costs, worsening Italy's economic strain and diplomatic isolation. Ultimately, Mussolini abandoned his earlier alignment with Britain and France, opting instead for a strategic alliance with other militarized, nationalist economies—Nazi Germany and Imperial Japan. This alliance, formalized as the Rome-Berlin-Tokyo Axis, was rooted in shared ideological and economic priorities: territorial expansion, economic nationalism, and the rejection of liberal democratic norms. Together, these partnerships laid the groundwork for the global conflict that erupted in World War II.

In contrast, anti-fascist economic justice promotes inclusive, democratic systems that value international cooperation, protect workers' rights, and prioritize social equity. It rejects the exclusionary logic of economic nationalism and instead supports economic models grounded in solidarity, accountability, and peace.

Contemporary anti-fascist economic thinking also aligns with efforts to move beyond both unregulated corporate capitalism and authoritarian state capitalism. It embraces stakeholder capitalism, which seeks to balance the interests of workers, communities, the environment, and future generations—not just shareholders. The post-fascist transition in Europe and Asia marked a profound shift in economic governance, labor protections, and welfare policies.

Table 5.2 outlines these key contrasts between pre-1945 fascist economic systems—including those in Italy, Germany, Spain, Portugal, and Japan—and their post-fascist, anti-fascist alternatives. These include Germany's Social Market Economy, Italy's Welfare State, Spain and Portugal's Market Liberalization, and Japan's model of State-Guided Capitalism.

Prior to 1945, fascist regimes maintained centralized economic control, aligning industries with state priorities—especially military expansion—while suppressing labor organizing and civil society. Infrastructure was militarized, trade was constrained by protectionist barriers and financial institutions operated under strict state supervision. Education systems served as tools of ideological indoctrination, while access to social services was highly conditional, often restricted by political loyalty or racial identity.

In stark contrast to fascist-era economies, post-fascist models embraced democratized market systems that reshaped governance, labor protections, and socioeconomic structures. Germany's *Soziale Marktwirtschaft* (Social Market Economy) combined free-market principles with strong worker rights, progressive taxation, and robust public investment. In Japan, state-directed industrial policies supported technological innovation and global economic integration. Meanwhile, Italy, Spain, and Portugal pursued market liberalization alongside expansive welfare programs and universal healthcare, reflecting a shift toward more inclusive and equitable societies. These transformations underscored a clear departure from authoritarian control, aligning economic systems with democratic governance and international cooperation.

Table 5.2: Fascist vs. Post-Fascist Economic Systems

ASPECT	FASCIST STATE CORPORATISM (MUSSOLINI, HITLER, FRANCO, ETC.)	POST-FASCIST MODELS (ITALY, GERMANY, JAPAN, ETC. POST-1945)
GOV'T ROLE IN ECONOMY	Centralized, state-led capitalism focused on military production.	Mixed economies balancing markets and state welfare.
WORKER RIGHTS & WELFARE	Unions banned; selective welfare; worker protections removed.	Strong labor rights, universal welfare, and public services.
GROWTH MODEL	Autarky, militarization, and expansionist economics.	Trade-driven growth and international cooperation.

INDUSTRY OWNERSHIP	Private sector under state control; key sectors nationalized.	Private ownership with government regulation.
TRADE & GLOBALIZATION	Isolationist, protectionist policies.	Global integration and free trade (e.g., EU, WTO).
TECH & INDUSTRY	War-focused innovation; military-industrial complex.	Civilian tech, public R&D, and export-led development.
BANKING & FINANCE	State-controlled banking for regime goals.	Regulated markets with central bank oversight.
AGRICULTURE	Favoring loyal landowners; centralized control.	Agrarian reforms and support for small farmers.
WEALTH DISTRIBUTION	Benefits for elites; high inequality.	Progressive taxation and growing middle class.
INFRASTRUCTURE	Militarized projects (e.g., roads for war logistics).	Civilian-focused investment in cities and services.
EDUCATION	Indoctrination promoting nationalism and obedience.	Public education promoting critical thought and democracy.
HEALTHCARE	Restricted to regime-favored groups.	Universal systems with equal access for all.
HOUSING & SOCIAL SERVICES	Politicized housing; minimal social aid.	Affordable housing and broader social safety nets.

WOMEN'S ROLES	Domestic roles promoted; workforce restricted.	Encouraged full employment and gender equality.
MILITARY SPENDING	High defense budgets; economy geared for war.	Reduced military budgets; focus on social development.
POLITICAL CONTROL OF ECONOMY	Totalitarian command over industry and resources.	Democratic economic governance with public input.

The post-World War II economic restructuring not only rebuilt war-torn nations but also embedded social and participatory values rooted in anti-fascist ideals. Germany's Social Market Economy exemplifies this balanced approach—combining free-market capitalism, which fosters competition and entrepreneurship, with robust social policies, including welfare programs, universal healthcare, labor protections, and public infrastructure. This hybrid model promotes sustainable growth, societal resilience, and inclusive prosperity.

Across post-war Europe, similar approaches took root. Cooperative and social enterprise models flourished, particularly in Italy, Spain, and the Nordic countries, strengthening local ownership, worker participation, and community engagement. In post-authoritarian Latin American contexts such as Argentina, Brazil, and Uruguay, the rise of solidarity economies and cooperative businesses addressed long-standing inequalities and expanded economic inclusion.

These examples collectively illustrate how anti-fascist economic justice continues to inform alternative development pathways—ones that prioritize democracy, equity, and human dignity alongside economic progress.

Together, these diverse economic approaches reflect the enduring influence of anti-fascist economic justice. They demonstrate that prosperity need not come at the cost of equity—that democratic, socially responsible economies can thrive when built on foundations of inclusion, accountability, and shared well-being.

Anti-Fascism and Critical Education

Russian President Vladimir Putin once stated, "Wars are won by teachers" (Stanley, 2024), acknowledging the profound power of education in shaping society, ideology, and national identity. However, the crucial question remains: who controls education, and to what end? Throughout history, authoritarian regimes have sought to limit knowledge, restrict intellectual freedom, and enforce ideological conformity—key strategies of fascist control (Giroux, 2018). In contrast, anti-fascist education champions critical thinking, historical awareness, and the ability to challenge oppressive structures, empowering individuals to recognize and resist authoritarianism.

In *Teaching Anti-Fascism: A Critical Pedagogy for Civic Engagement*, Michael Vavrus (2022) suggests various approaches, methods and topics that should be included in an anti-fascist critical education. Among them, are historical analyses of fascist movements, critical media literacy to counter propaganda and misinformation, the study of systemic oppression and authoritarian tendencies, and pedagogical strategies that emphasize civic engagement and democratic participation. Vavrus also advocates for interdisciplinary approaches that connect historical patterns of fascism with contemporary political and social issues, encouraging students to critically analyze power structures, challenge exclusionary ideologies, and develop the skills necessary for active resistance against authoritarianism.

As an instructor myself, I recognize the importance of integrating practical tools and concrete examples into educational curricula across various disciplines. By incorporating relevant case studies, interdisciplinary methodologies, and diverse teaching strategies, educators can effectively promote critical thinking and civic engagement among students. These approaches underscore the necessity of understanding both historical and contemporary manifestations of fascist ideologies, analyzing authoritarian structures, and advocating for democratic principles. Employing real-world examples and participatory educational techniques empowers students to adopt an informed and proactive stance against oppression, misinformation, and systemic injustice.

Table 5.3 outlines key topics and strategies for teaching antifascist perspectives across academic disciplines. It emphasizes the importance of interdisciplinary approaches that not only build historical awareness but also cultivate critical thinking, civic responsibility, and democratic engagement. By integrating antifascist content into fields such as history, political science, literature, philosophy, and media studies, educators can help students recognize the ideological patterns and social conditions that give rise to authoritarianism. The table highlights a variety of effective pedagogical methods—including debate-based learning, media literacy training, experiential simulations, and the analysis of primary sources—all designed to engage learners actively and equip them with the analytical tools needed to identify and resist fascist tendencies in both historical and contemporary contexts.

Table 5.3: Critical Anti-Fascist Education

DISCIPLINE	KEY TOPICS & EXAMPLES	SUGGESTED TEACHING METHODS
HISTORY	Comparative history of fascism and anti-fascist movements (Mussolini, Hitler, Franco, contemporary fascism)	Primary source analysis, historical documentaries, group discussions
POLITICAL SCIENCE	Authoritarianism, democracy, and civic engagement (democratic backsliding, populism)	Role-playing simulations, structured debates, case studies

SOCIOLOGY	Systemic oppression and resistance (racism, gender oppression, class struggles)	Intersectional analysis, service-learning projects, activist partnerships
MEDIA STUDIES	Propaganda, misinformation, and media literacy (fact-checking historical and contemporary propaganda)	Media literacy workshops, digital forensics exercises, social media analysis
PHILOSOPHY	Ethics, power, and democracy (Socratic seminars on ethical dilemmas in governance and resistance)	Philosophical dialogues, ethical case studies, student-led presentations
EDUCATION	Pedagogies of resistance and transformative education (student-led civic engagement projects)	Community-based learning, participatory action research, policy advocacy
LITERATURE	Literature as resistance and critique (Orwell's *1984*, Arendt's *The Origins of Totalitarianism*)	Literary analysis, thematic essays, performance-based interpretations
ECONOMICS	Economic roots of fascism and corporate influence (economic crises and authoritarianism)	Economic simulations, inequality mapping, corporate accountability research
LAW	Human rights, constitutional safeguards, and legal resistance (mock trials on human rights violations)	Legal analysis, courtroom simulations, human rights advocacy campaigns

PSYCHOLOGY	Psychological manipulation, groupthink, and authoritarian personality (Milgram, Zimbardo experiments)	Experiential learning, psychology experiments, critical reflections
ANTHROPOLOGY	Cultural identity, nationalism, and ethnonationalist ideologies (ethnographic studies on nationalism)	Fieldwork, cross-cultural comparisons, oral histories
ENVIRONMENTAL STUDIES	Eco-fascism, climate justice, and sustainability (activism projects countering eco-fascist narratives)	Project-based learning, environmental activism campaigns, policy discussions
MANAGEMENT	Ethical leadership and corporate resistance (business complicity in fascism, e.g., IBM & Nazi Germany)	Ethical case studies, leadership simulations, corporate social audits
BUSINESS ETHICS	Business ethics in political crises (corporate complicity in authoritarian regimes)	Debates on business ethics, stakeholder mapping, corporate complicity analysis
PUBLIC ADMINISTRATION	Democratic governance and resisting bureaucratic authoritarianism (comparative governance structures)	Public policy simulations, governance role-play, real-world case studies
CRIMINAL JUSTICE	Policing in authoritarian states and protecting civil rights (police	Restorative justice workshops, community policing research, legal case studies

	militarization, resistance movements)	
HEALTH SCIENCES	Public health as a human right, medical fascism, and bioethics (Nazi T4, Tuskegee Syphilis Study, forced sterilizations)	Bioethics case analysis, ethical role-play, policy reviews
INFORMATION TECHNOLOGY	Digital authoritarianism, cybersecurity, and surveillance capitalism (China's social credit system)	Cybersecurity simulations, ethical hacking workshops, surveillance policy debates
COMMUNICATION STUDIES	Rhetoric, propaganda, and resisting disinformation (deconstructing political speeches, media bias)	Rhetorical analysis, media literacy training, propaganda deconstruction exercises
ART & DESIGN	Art as resistance (political posters, graffiti, and activism, e.g., Banksy, Ai Weiwei)	Collaborative art projects, historical analysis of political posters, digital activism

Anti-fascist education and inclusive leadership training are inherently interconnected, as both underscore the essential roles of diversity, equity, and inclusion (DEI) in sustainable socio-economic development. Amid escalating authoritarian threats, cultivating critical thinking and innovative problem-solving necessitates leadership models that actively challenge oppressive frameworks and embrace pluralism. Bollinger's statement, "We're in the midst of an authoritarian takeover" (as cited in Goldstein & Gutkin, 2025), highlights the urgent need to equip leaders with strategies that mitigate democratic erosion. Lee Bollinger, a First Amendment scholar and former president of Columbia University, has consistently advocated for affirmative action and educational policies aligned with democratic values.

The Great Replacement theory, as described by Camus (2018), is a fascist conspiracy theory grounded in xenophobia and fearmongering, which fuels authoritarianism by rationalizing exclusionary policies and societal division. In contrast, inclusive, anti-fascist leadership education actively counters such narratives by emphasizing inclusion, equity, and the value of diverse perspectives. Higher Education Institutions (HEIs) that incorporate DEI principles into leadership training enhance democratic resilience, encourage innovation, and ensure human rights in societies are well-equipped to address contemporary socio-political challenges (Vissing, 2025).

Nevertheless, genuinely critical education refrains from dictating specific thoughts and instead prioritizes teaching learners how to think critically—an educational philosophy central to both Don Lorenzo Milani and Paulo Freire. Both educators explicitly rejected passive educational models intended to maintain existing social hierarchies, advocating instead for pedagogies rooted in critical analysis, inclusivity, and liberation.

At his small rural school in Barbiana, Don Milani rejected Italy's rigid and exclusionary education system, which systematically marginalized the poor and denied them meaningful access to learning. Instead, he built his pedagogy around the ethos of "I CARE," a profound statement of social responsibility and solidarity that stood in direct opposition to Mussolini's fascist motto *"Me ne frego"* (I don't care), which glorified apathy and blind obedience (Tavanti, 2024, pp. 114–117). Through this philosophy, Don Lorenzo Milani, instilled in his students a sense of moral duty and active engagement, transforming education into a tool for empowerment and justice.

One of his most famous works, *Lettera a una professoressa* (Milani, 1967), co-authored with his Barbiana students, directly criticized the Italian school system for perpetuating class-based inequalities. He argued that traditional education reinforced the status quo by privileging the children of elites while excluding working-class students through standardized testing and rote memorization. Instead, Don Milani promoted an education that empowered students to critically engage with the world and become active citizens.

Don Milani's commitment to conscience-based education extended beyond the classroom. He famously defended conscientious objectors, arguing that compulsory military service was a mechanism of state coercion that contradicted individual moral autonomy (Milani, 2008). His advocacy for students' right to dissent directly challenged the authoritarian structures of both the church and state, making his pedagogy inherently anti-fascist.

Paulo Freire's *Pedagogy of the Oppressed* (1970) created a framework for critical pedagogy, arguing that traditional education functions as a tool of oppression when it merely deposits information into students without engaging their capacity for reflection and agency. Freire's problem-posing model of education was designed to break this cycle by fostering a critical consciousness (*conscientização*), which enables individuals to perceive and challenge systems of injustice (Freire, 2000).

Freire's method, developed through his work with illiterate farmers in Brazil, sought to transform students from passive recipients of knowledge into active participants in their own liberation. Through dialogue and participatory learning, students analyzed their lived experiences in relation to historical and political structures, recognizing how economic and social forces shaped their realities (McLaren, 2022). This process directly opposed fascist educational models, which rely on rote obedience and discourage independent thought.

Freire's approach to literacy education also had political implications. By teaching oppressed communities to read and write in ways that connected their learning to their material conditions, Freire's work became a direct challenge to authoritarian regimes in Latin America. His ideas were so threatening to the Brazilian military dictatorship that he was imprisoned and later exiled for his radical approach to education (Gadotti, 1994).

Anti-fascist education demands a critical and honest engagement with history. It ensures that injustices like colonialism, racism, and fascism are neither forgotten nor rewritten. This stands in sharp contrast to today's authoritarian trends—such as book bans in places like Florida, driven by opposition to Critical Race Theory (CRT) (Apple, 2021). These bans, which target books about racism, gender, and historical injustice, echo the censorship tactics of fascist regimes that aimed to control public thought. CRT itself has been misrepresented as a threat to national identity, when in fact it examines how systemic racism operates in legal and institutional systems. It promotes historical awareness and helps guard against the rise of authoritarian narratives (Delgado & Stefancic, 2017). The backlash against CRT is part of a broader effort to suppress critical thinking by casting truth-telling as dangerous or unpatriotic.

To further highlight the contrast between fascist and antifascist approaches to education, Table 5.4 outlines their defining characteristics. Fascist education models emphasize obedience, uniformity, and ideological control, reinforcing hierarchical power structures by suppressing critical inquiry. In contrast, antifascist education encourages independent thought, inclusivity, and civic engagement, equipping individuals with the tools to challenge oppression and uphold democratic values. Understanding these opposing paradigms is essential in recognizing how education can either sustain authoritarian rule or serve as a catalyst for liberation and social justice.

Education functions as both a mechanism of control and a means of empowerment, depending on its guiding philosophy, institutional framework, and implementation. Historically, authoritarian regimes have manipulated education to enforce ideological conformity, erase historical truths, and limit intellectual freedom. By contrast, democratic and antifascist education cultivates historical awareness, critical analysis, and active participation in society, enabling individuals to resist authoritarian tendencies.

Analyzing key aspects of education—such as curriculum design, teaching methodologies, censorship policies, academic freedom, and institutional oversight—reveals the underlying dynamics that distinguish fascist, and antifascist approaches in schools and educational programs. This comparison helps identify whether an educational system reinforces authoritarian control or fosters critical thinking, democratic engagement, and intellectual freedom.

Authoritarian systems prioritize nationalism, indoctrination, and suppression of dissent, shaping education into a tool for maintaining control. On the contrary, antifascist education champions inquiry-driven learning, diverse perspectives, and media literacy, to give learners the capacity to question political, social and cultural assumptions.

Table 5.4: Anti-Fascist Mindsets in Education

ASPECT	EDUCATION WITH A FASCIST MINDSET	EDUCATION WITH AN ANTI-FASCIST MINDSET
PURPOSE OF EDUCATION	Indoctrination, loyalty to the state, suppression of dissent	Critical thinking, empowerment, and democratic engagement
TEACHING APPROACH	Rote memorization, passive absorption of state-approved content	Dialogical learning, problem-posing education (Freire, Milani)
ROLE OF THE TEACHER	Authoritative figure, enforcer of conformity	Facilitator of inquiry and discussion, guiding the students by the side
STUDENT AGENCY	Submissive, discouraged from questioning authority	Encouraged to question and critically analyze information
CURRICULUM CONTENT	Nationalistic, sanitized history, exclusion of marginalized perspectives	Inclusive history, emphasis on social justice and diverse perspectives
APPROACH TO HISTORY	Revisionist, glorifies the state, erases inconvenient truths	Confronts historical injustices, promotes accountability

CITIZENSHIP MODEL	Blind patriotism, obedience to authority	Active citizenship, responsibility for social change
VIEW OF DISSENT	Criminalized, seen as a threat to order	Valued as essential for democracy and progress
OUTCOME	Reinforces hierarchical power, limits democratic aspirations	Develops engaged, critical, and socially responsible citizens

Educators like Don Lorenzo Milani and Paulo Freire exemplify the anti-fascist approach, advocating for education that equips students with the analytical skills necessary to recognize and challenge authoritarianism in all its forms. Education rooted in critical analysis, historical accuracy, and social justice is the antidote to fascist manipulation. Whether through Don Milani's fight for education as a tool of liberation, Freire's insistence on consciousness-raising, or CRT's challenge to structural inequalities, anti-fascist education defends the right to know, to question, and to resist. Without it, societies risk regressing into obedience-based, exclusionary, and hierarchical structures that authoritarianism relies upon to sustain itself.

Anti-Fascism and Liberating Religion

Religion has historically functioned as both a force of liberation and a tool of oppression. While anti-fascist religious movements champion justice, human dignity, and the emancipation of the oppressed, ideologies like Christian nationalism and clerical fascism have aligned with authoritarianism, using faith to justify exclusion, nationalism, and hierarchical control. The contrast between these interpretations is stark. One seeks to empower, while the other demands submission to state and religious authority.

The deep entanglement of evangelical Christianity with American politics illustrates this dynamic. Ronald Reagan's presidency marked a turning point in conservative Christian activism, forging an alliance with the religious right that continues today. Figures like Jerry Falwell and the Moral Majority mobilized voters around issues such as opposition to abortion and school prayer, framing America as a divinely chosen nation in need of moral restoration (Martin, 2005). This fusion of religion and politics paved the way for the rise of Christian nationalism, which reached its most explicit form in the elections of Donald Trump.

As Whitehead and Perry explain in *Taking America Back for God* (2020), Christian nationalism—a movement that fuses American identity with the belief that Christianity should define the nation—became a driving force behind Trump's electoral success. Unlike Reagan, who maintained a more personal, traditional Christian image, Trump's appeal was rooted in his willingness to position himself as a defender of evangelical interests, despite his personal life being at odds with religious conservatism. His presidency capitalized on Christian nationalist fears of secularism, globalism, and progressive social change, rallying support around issues such as conservative Supreme Court appointments, religious freedom protections, and opposition to abortion.

This movement extended beyond electoral politics. The January 6, 2021, attack on the U.S. Capitol was rife with Christian nationalist symbols, prayers, and rhetoric, reinforcing Whitehead and Perry's argument that Christian nationalism is not merely about religious belief but about a broader effort to reshape American democracy around an exclusionary, authoritarian vision (Whitehead & Perry, 2020). The movement weaponizes faith to legitimize political power, suppress dissent, and reinforce racial and cultural hierarchies—paralleling historical examples of clerical fascism in Italy and Spain.

Fascist regimes have long recognized the power of religious belief, often co-opting it to consolidate control. Mussolini's Italy, Hitler's Germany, and even Stalin's Soviet Union cultivated political religions that demanded absolute loyalty to the state, replacing pluralism and individual conscience with a sacralized nationalist ideology (Pollard,

1998). Historian Emilio Gentile describes political religions as systems that blend state authority with sacred narratives, making dissent a form of heresy. Similarly, theologian Dorothee Sölle coined the term Christofascism to describe the use of Christianity to enforce authoritarianism, turning faith into a tool of oppression based on race, gender, and class. In Mussolini's case, elements of the Catholic Church aligned with fascism, suppressing independent Catholic movements and promoting obedience to the regime.

Today, Christian nationalism in the U.S. and Europe follows this legacy, advocating for the fusion of state and religious power under the banner of "spiritual warfare." The rhetoric of restoring Christian values is used to justify exclusionary policies, voter suppression, book bans, and attacks on immigrants—tactics eerily reminiscent of past fascist strategies (O'Donnell, 2020).

In contrast, anti-fascist religious movements challenge authoritarian control and advocate for social justice. Don Milani, alongside fellow Florentine priests like Don Ernesto Balducci, rejected the clerical complicity in fascism, arguing that true faith compels individuals to resist unjust authority rather than submit unquestioningly. In his *Lettera ai Giudici* (Letter to the Judges) written during his trial for defending conscientious objectors, Don Milani declared, "Obedience is no longer a virtue but the most deceptive of temptations" (Milani, 1971). His belief that faith should serve the marginalized, not the powerful, directly opposed fascist ideologies that demanded unquestioning obedience.

Similarly, the emergence of liberation theology in Latin America in the mid-20th century explicitly rejected religion as a tool for political domination. Figures like Gustavo Gutiérrez in Peru and Óscar Romero in El Salvador preached that faith must align with the poor and the oppressed rather than serve ruling elites. Their teachings directly challenged military dictatorships that had embraced Christian nationalist rhetoric to justify state violence and economic exploitation. Romero, assassinated for his advocacy, exemplified how anti-fascist religious leaders have been targeted for opposing authoritarian rule.

Fascist ideologies thrive on obedience, fear, and moral suppression. Anti-fascist religious traditions, in contrast, emphasize critical thinking, inclusion, and resistance to oppression. Whether through Don Milani's advocacy for conscience, the liberation theology of Latin America, or contemporary resistance against religious authoritarianism, the message remains clear—faith should never be a tool for exclusion and domination but rather a force for freedom, dignity, and social transformation.

Religious belief systems can shape vastly different approaches to power, authority, and social justice, fostering either a conservative (pro-fascist) or liberating (anti-fascist) mindset. A conservative religious perspective, closely tied to authoritarianism, emphasizes obedience to religious and political leadership, enforces hierarchical structures, and upholds exclusionary moral codes that reinforce nationalism, traditionalism, and social conformity. It seeks to preserve the status quo, portraying dissent as a destabilizing force and using faith to justify the subjugation of marginalized groups.

This pro-fascist religious mindset merges religious identity with nationalism, demanding absolute loyalty to authority while discouraging critical thought. It legitimizes oppressive policies by advocating for close ties between religious institutions and the state, presenting them as divinely ordained. In this framework, tradition and order take precedence over individual rights, and any challenge to authority is framed as a threat to societal and moral stability.

In contrast, a liberating religious perspective—rooted in social justice, inclusion, and critical inquiry—prioritizes human dignity, moral autonomy, and active resistance to oppression. It aligns faith with the empowerment of the poor and disenfranchised, challenging unjust authority and fostering solidarity across cultural and social divisions. This anti-fascist approach to religion sees faith as a force for justice and compassion, encouraging believers to question oppressive systems rather than blindly submit to them. It supports the separation of religion and state to prevent theocratic rule and acknowledges historical injustices carried out in the name of faith. Rather than idealizing the past, it promotes transformation, progress, and the pursuit of equality.

Table 5.5 illustrates the stark contrast between these two approaches, showing how religious ideology can either entrench authoritarianism or serve as a tool for liberation and social change. Throughout history, religion has been both a justification for exclusionary power structures and a driving force behind resistance to tyranny.

Table 5.5: Anti-Fascist Religious Mindsets

Aspect	Conservative Religious (Pro-Fascist) Mindset	Liberating Religious (Anti-Fascist) Mindset
View of Authority	Absolute obedience to religious and political leaders	Challenges unjust authority, prioritizes moral conscience
Role of Religion	Upholds nationalism, traditional values, and social hierarchy	Advocates for social justice, inclusion, and human dignity
Moral Perspective	Strict moral codes used to regulate behavior and exclude "outsiders"	Emphasizes compassion, solidarity, and human rights
Approach to Dissent	Dissent is punished or suppressed	Dissent is a moral obligation against injustice
Relationship to the State	Supports close alliance between church and state	Advocates separation of religion and state to prevent oppression
Treatment of Marginalized Groups	Reinforces existing social hierarchies and exclusions	Prioritizes uplifting the oppressed and marginalized

Historical Narrative	Glorifies a mythologized national or religious past	Acknowledges past injustices and promotes historical truth
Ultimate Goal	Preservation of order, tradition, and authority	Liberation, justice, and transformation of society

Understanding these divergent roles is crucial for analyzing the intersection of faith, politics, and social control, as religious belief systems have historically played powerful roles in both sustaining authoritarian rule and fostering democratic resistance. While pro-fascist religious ideologies have been used to justify colonialism, authoritarianism, and exclusionary nationalism, anti-fascist religious movements have offered a counter-narrative rooted in justice and human dignity. Examples include Don Milani's advocacy for conscientious objection in post-war Italy and the emergence of liberation theology in Latin America, which aligned the Church with the struggles of the poor and marginalized. These contrasting religious mindsets illustrate how faith can either reinforce oppressive systems or challenge them. When rooted in critical thought and ethical responsibility, religion becomes a transformative force—supporting human rights, equity, and social change rather than submission to unjust power.

Countering Fascism

Resisting fascism requires a multifaceted approach that addresses its political, social, economic, and cultural dimensions. Expanding on Mason's (2021) *How to Stop Fascism: History, Ideology, Resistance*, which outlines key strategies for countering authoritarianism, I propose the following comprehensive set of antifascist strategies:

1. **Strengthening Democratic Institutions** – Upholding the rule of law, protecting judicial independence, and ensuring free and fair elections to prevent the erosion of democratic norms.

2. **Advancing Critical and Antifascist Education** – Incorporating historical analysis and media literacy into educational curricula to help individuals recognize propaganda, resist disinformation, and understand the dangers of authoritarian ideologies.

3. **Countering Disinformation and Fake News Narratives** – Supporting fact-checking initiatives, independent journalism, and public awareness campaigns to dismantle conspiracy theories and reduce political radicalization.

4. **Building Inclusive Social and Political Movements** – Uniting diverse communities in coalitions that resist exclusionary ideologies, promote human rights, and safeguard pluralism through civic activism and grassroots organizing.

5. **Addressing Economic Inequality and Social Grievances** – Implementing policies that promote economic justice, fair wages, and wealth redistribution to counteract the economic anxieties that fascists exploit to fuel division and scapegoating.

6. **Encouraging Intellectual and Cultural Resistance** – Supporting artists, writers, filmmakers, and scholars who critically engage with authoritarianism, preserve historical memory, and use creative expression to challenge oppressive narratives.

7. **Liberating Religion from Political Manipulation** – Preventing the co-optation of religious institutions by authoritarian regimes and promoting interpretations that emphasize social justice, inclusion, and human rights.

8. **Mobilizing Legal and Institutional Protections** – Enforcing anti-discrimination laws, prosecuting hate crimes, and creating safeguards against the abuse of state power to curb authoritarian encroachment.

9. **Strengthening International Solidarity** – Collaborating with global democratic movements, human rights organizations, and international institutions to counter authoritarianism on a transnational scale.

Resisting fascism requires continuous commitment to justice, democracy, and human dignity. It demands vigilance, education, and collective action to prevent authoritarian ideologies from taking root. The resurgence of fascist movements is not inevitable but arises from specific economic, political, and social conditions that create openings for authoritarianism. As Walden Bello (2019) argues in *Counterrevolution and How to Counter Fascism*, economic insecurity, fear, and cultural resentment fuel reactionary movements, eroding democratic institutions. Recognizing these dynamics—along with disinformation, surveillance-driven suppression of dissent, and the manipulation of security concerns—is critical in resisting authoritarianism.

Countering fascism requires a broad coalition of individuals, communities, and institutions committed to defending democratic principles. Bello (2024) emphasizes that effective resistance must extend beyond electoral politics to include grassroots activism, international solidarity, and institutional reform. Similarly, Traverso (2019) highlights the deep connection between modern far-right populism and classical fascist ideologies, underscoring the need for updated antifascist strategies that address contemporary threats, particularly in the digital age. Social media and algorithm-driven content have made it easier for authoritarian movements to spread disinformation and manipulate public perception, making digital literacy and critical thinking essential tools of resistance.

To combat these modern threats, antifascist efforts must challenge online radicalization, counteract reactionary narratives, and promote inclusive democratic discourse. By adapting resistance strategies to the realities of today's political and technological landscape, societies can better prevent authoritarian forces from gaining traction.

Ultimately, the survival of democracy hinges on our active engagement—intellectually, politically, and socially. As Martin Luther King Jr. powerfully reminded us in a sermon delivered in Selma, Alabama, on March 8, 1965, the day after "Bloody Sunday": "A man dies when he refuses to stand up for that which is right... for justice... for that which is true." Often paraphrased as, "Our lives begin to end the day we become silent about things that matter," this message remains a timeless call to action. Confronting fascism demands more than opposition—it requires a steadfast commitment to justice, truth, and equality. History makes clear that silence and passivity embolden authoritarianism. Only through vigilance, moral courage, and collective responsibility can we fortify democratic institutions and ensure they endure from within.

| 6 |

DECODING TECHNO-FACISM

"The power that surveillance capitalism grants to a handful of tech companies is unprecedented. It creates a society where those who control the data control the people—an invisible form of coercion and social engineering that is more insidious than traditional fascism."

— Shoshana Zuboff, *The Age of Surveillance Capitalism*, 2019

The rise of techno-fascism is deeply embedded in the convergence of technological innovation, corporate dominance, and authoritarian governance. While technology has long been celebrated as a force for democratization and social progress, history reveals its dual nature—serving not only as a tool for empowerment but also as a mechanism for surveillance, control, and political manipulation. Historian Janis Mimura (2011) explores this dynamic in *Planning for Empire*, analyzing how Japan's Pre-World War II bureaucratic elites harnessed industrial and technological advancements to centralize authority. The patterns she identifies bear striking parallels to today's corporate-controlled digital landscape, where technology companies shape not only economies but also political discourse and governance structures.

In contemporary society, the emergence of techno-fascism has been further explored by Kyle Chayka (2025) in *The New Yorker*, particularly through the influence of Elon Musk on digital governance and political power. Chayka argues that Musk represents a new kind of tech leader—one who blends libertarian ideals with authoritarian control, using platforms like X (formerly Twitter) to manipulate public debate, discredit opponents, and consolidate digital power. Unlike traditional forms of political authoritarianism, this new iteration of techno-fascism embeds control mechanisms directly into digital infrastructure, ensuring that technology itself becomes both the medium and the enforcer of ideological dominance.

The historical precedents of fascist regimes, including Nazi Germany and Mussolini's Italy, reveal how industrial partnerships played a crucial role in fueling militarization and maintaining social control. Today, the rise of technocrats—engineers, data scientists, and corporate executives—has shifted this dynamic from state-centered authoritarianism to a corporate-state hybrid, where algorithms and digital monopolies increasingly dictate governance. Shoshana Zuboff (2019) explores this transformation in *The Age of Surveillance Capitalism*, arguing that digital platforms have evolved beyond mere economic entities into governance structures that shape political realities, mediate public discourse, and redefine the boundaries of permissible thought.

To grasp the contemporary expressions of techno-fascism, its impact on authoritarian and populist leaders, and its broader consequences for democratic values, we must examine the role of Silicon Valley's libertarian ethos—particularly among figures like Peter Thiel and the so-called "PayPal Mafia" (Soni, 2022).

According to Zuboff (2019), "Instrumentarian power knows and shapes human behavior toward others' ends. It is a new species of power that works through the medium of digital instrumentation to manipulate social relations and modify individual actions at scale" (p. 17). These dynamics highlight how technofascist tendencies emerge within a broader context of algorithmic control and data-driven governance.

This ideological framework fuels a form of techno-authoritarianism in which power is centralized in the hands of unelected tech elites who use algorithmic governance to consolidate influence. However, techno-fascism does not operate in isolation. It is part of a broader range of techno-driven governance models, each shaping the interplay between technology, power, and society. Recognizing these related concepts is essential to understanding how technology can be wielded for control, manipulated for populist appeal, or leveraged for nationalistic and economic dominance (Hillman, 2022).

Table 6.1 defines key terms related to techno-fascism, an extreme form of digital authoritarianism that reflects overlapping trends such as techno-authoritarianism, techno-populism, and other evolving models of governance shaped by technology. These terms illustrate the continuum from technocracy—ruled by technical experts—to cyberocracy, where information systems and digital infrastructures increasingly influence or control political decision-making. The table includes both foundational and contemporary concepts that predate modern high-tech developments but have shaped current forms of technologically enabled power. The table also includes examples that may be interpreted differently depending on the reader's perspective yet still illustrate key expressions and tendencies commonly associated with techno-fascist dynamics.

Table 6.1: Techno-Fascism Related Terms

TERM	DEFINITION	EXAMPLES
TECHNO-FASCISM	The use of technology by authoritarian leaders or regimes to control populations and suppress dissent.	China's social credit system, AI-driven mass surveillance in autocratic states.

TECHNO-AUTHORITARIANISM	The integration of technology with state power to enforce political control, often sidelining democratic institutions.	Palantir's predictive policing, AI-powered censorship in authoritarian regimes.
TECHNO-POPULISM	A political movement that fuses populist rhetoric with technology-driven governance, often positioning digital platforms as tools for direct democracy.	The Five Star Movement in Italy, Elon Musk's Twitter/X policy shifts.
TECHNO-CAPITALISM	The dominance of digital and platform-based economies in shaping economic structures, often concentrating wealth and power in a few tech corporations.	Amazon's monopolization of e-commerce, Google's data economy.
TECHNO-NATIONALISM	The use of technology to advance national interests, often through state-supported digital industries and protectionist policies.	China's Made in China 2025 initiative, U.S. restrictions on Huawei.
TECHNO-PROGRESSIVISM	A belief that technological advancements should be harnessed for social good, emphasizing ethical AI, environmental sustainability, and human rights.	European Union's AI Act, open-source technology movements.
TECHNO-LIBERTARIANISM	The advocacy of minimal government intervention in digital innovation, often prioritizing free-market approaches to tech regulation.	Peter Thiel's opposition to government oversight of tech, cryptocurrency anarcho-capitalism.

| TECHNO-UTOPIANISM | The idea that technology alone can solve all human problems and lead to a future of abundance and equality. | Silicon Valley's transhumanist movements, AI-driven governance models. |

Oligarchs for Algorithmic Governance

The growing influence of Silicon Valley executives in state affairs marks a transition from democratic governance to an era where digital oligarchs exert direct influence over policymaking. The second Trump presidency has intensified this trend, with figures like Elon Musk and Peter Thiel shaping governmental policies through financial and ideological support (Chayka, 2025; Tscheschlok, 2024). The merging of corporate and political power is not new, but the scale and sophistication of digital technologies have transformed governance into a system increasingly dictated by AI-driven decision-making, mass data collection, and predictive analytics. This shift raises serious concerns about democratic accountability, as unelected tech executives wield disproportionate power over public discourse, electoral outcomes, and national security policies.

DiResta (2024), in *Invisible Rulers: The People Who Turn Lies Into Reality,* observes how Musk's acquisition of Twitter (now X) showcases the dangers of algorithmic governance. With control over one of the world's largest social media platforms, he has not only influenced public debate but has also allowed the unchecked spread of disinformation and political propaganda under the guise of "free speech" (Lewandowsky, 2025).

Disinformation: *Intentional | False or misleading | Created to deceive.* Disinformation has become a powerful weapon for authoritarian leaders, extremist groups, and political operatives. Its deliberate aim is to manipulate public opinion, sow distrust, and destabilize democratic institutions. Often crafted to appear credible and shared through coordinated campaigns, disinformation thrives in the digital environment where speed and scale amplify its reach.

Misinformation: *Unintentional | False or inaccurate | Shared without intent to deceive.* While misinformation lacks the intent to mislead, it still poses a serious threat to public understanding. It often spreads rapidly through social media, private messaging apps, and online communities, unintentionally reinforcing falsehoods. By echoing and amplifying disinformation, misinformation contributes to a fragmented information landscape where truth becomes harder to discern.

Studies have demonstrated the alarming effectiveness of these tactics; a well-known MIT study found that false information spreads up to four times faster than factual news on social media platforms (Vosoughi, Roy, & Aral, 2018). This phenomenon enables political actors to manipulate public opinion at an unprecedented scale.

Nobel laureate Maria Ressa, a journalist and founder of Rappler, has documented extensively how disinformation campaigns were used by the Duterte regime in the Philippines to silence dissent and manufacture public consent for extrajudicial killings. Ressa has consistently warned that social media platforms, particularly Facebook (Meta), have facilitated the erosion of democracy by failing to curb the spread of state-sponsored propaganda. Facebook's algorithm prioritizes engagement over the accuracy, rewarding outrage and polarization, which in turn fuels political extremes.

In *How to Stand Up to a Dictator,* Ressa (2022) argues that the unchecked power of tech platforms has fundamentally altered the way people perceive truth, creating a system where lies travel faster than facts. She states, "When you allow lies to spread faster than facts, the world turns upside down. The platform that delivers the news also delivers poison" (p. 112). This observation highlights the dangers of algorithmic amplification in shaping public discourse and its role in enabling authoritarian regimes to manipulate public perception at an unprecedented scale. Without structural reforms and greater accountability, these platforms will continue to serve as tools for autocratic control rather than democratic empowerment. The consequences of this algorithmic manipulation extend beyond the Philippines; in Myanmar, Facebook was instrumental in the dissemination of hate speech that fueled the Rohingya genocide, demonstrating the platform's global role in enabling authoritarian violence (Mozur, 2018).

Similarly, as detailed in *The Contrarian: Peter Thiel and Silicon Valley's Pursuit of Power* (Chafkin, 2021), Thiel's Palantir Technologies shows how some high-tech companies can increasingly operate as extensions of state security apparatuses. By providing AI-driven surveillance and intelligence services to governments, Palantir underscores the deep entanglement between private tech enterprises and public security infrastructure. Palantir's data analytics platforms have been used for predictive policing, immigration enforcement, and counterterrorism, raising concerns about mass surveillance and racial profiling. Benkler (2006) highlights how these developments undermine democratic institutions, shifting power away from elected representatives and toward unaccountable corporate executives who control the flow of information and intelligence.

In *The Tech Coup: How to Save Democracy from Silicon Valley,* Marietje Schaake (2024) underscores the urgency of addressing Big Tech's influence, stating, "We must refuse to be guinea pigs." She argues that the unchecked power of technology companies has led to a scenario where "the digitization of everything has enabled the weaponization of everything," highlighting the pervasive nature of technological threats (Schaake, 2024). Schaake emphasizes that this is not a stance against technology itself but a call to preserve democratic values in the face of rapid technological advancement

The role of artificial intelligence in governance further complicates this landscape. As O'Neil (2016) warns in *Weapons of Math Destruction*, algorithmic decision-making often reinforces systemic biases, disproportionately targeting marginalized communities while insulating the elite from accountability. Predictive policing algorithms, for instance, are trained on historically biased data, leading to over-policing of Black and Brown communities while largely ignoring white-collar crime and corruption. AI-driven hiring processes and loan approval systems have also been found to replicate and exacerbate racial and gender disparities, demonstrating how algorithmic governance prioritizes efficiency and profitability over fairness and social justice (Eubanks, 2018).

Techno-Democracy vs. Techno-fascism

We are living through the Fourth Industrial Revolution (4IR), a transformative era where high-tech industries increasingly shape every sphere of modern life. Driven by data, automation, and interconnected intelligence, this revolution reconfigures not only economic systems but also political power structures and civil liberties (Sieber-Gasser & Ghibellini, 2021; Brito & Castillo, 2023).

Hélène Landemore, Lucy Bernholz, and Rob Reich argue in *Digital Technology and Democratic Theory* (2021), digital innovations offer democratic promise: they can enhance participation, increase transparency, and decentralize decision-making. Yet these same tools can also become instruments of control. Steven Feldstein, in *The Rise of Digital Repression* (2021), details how authoritarian regimes use technology to surveil, manipulate, and silence dissent.

Christian Fuchs (2022) advances this critique in *Digital Fascism*, showing how digital platforms—driven by algorithmic logic—amplify extremism, nationalism, and hate. These systems cultivate echo chambers, propagate misinformation, and commodify outrage, distorting public discourse and weakening democratic institutions. Martin Moore (2018), in *Democracy Hacked*, warns of a deeper erosion: the weaponization of digital infrastructure for information warfare, data mining, microtargeting, and civic manipulation. In his view, democracy itself is being "hacked"—not only by foreign actors or authoritarian states but also by corporate and political elites leveraging opaque systems of control.

At this pivotal 4IR moment, humanity must decide how technology will shape our collective future. Will it serve democratic renewal or deepen authoritarian control? Urgent reforms are needed to protect electoral integrity, rebuild civic trust, and ensure that the digital age advances freedom rather than suppresses it.

Techno-democracy: This trajectory and priority envisions a future where technology serves the public good. In this model, digital innovations are harnessed to strengthen participatory governance, enhance transparency and accountability, and decentralize decision-making processes. It is a vision rooted in the empowerment of citizens—where civic engagement is not only protected but actively encouraged through open, inclusive technological systems.

Techno-fascism: This contrasting choice represents a future where technology becomes a tool of control. This path is marked by widespread surveillance, digital repression, and algorithmic manipulation designed to influence behavior and suppress dissent. Power becomes increasingly centralized in authoritarian regimes, while civil liberties erode and public trust collapses under the weight of manipulation and fear.

This is the defining choice of our time. Whether we will build technological systems that empower people or allow them to be used for control, division, and domination. This struggle unfolds across every domain of digital life. Table 6.1 illustrates how key technologies can either strengthen democracy or fuel digital fascism, depending on their application. It highlights the dual potential of digital tools—to enable broad civic empowerment (techno-democracy) or to serve narrow authoritarian interests (techno-fascism), echoing what Levitsky and Ziblatt (2023) describe as the "tyranny of the minority."

Table 6.2: Technology & Governance Outcomes

Technology	Techno-Democracy Outcome	Techno-Fascism Outcome
Social Media Platforms & Algorithms	Open platforms for civic engagement, decentralized discourse, grassroots mobilization	Algorithmic manipulation, mass propaganda, censorship, digital echo chambers fostering authoritarian control
Artificial Intelligence (AI)	AI-driven participatory governance, predictive policymaking for social good	AI-powered mass surveillance, automated repression, and predictive policing
Blockchain	Decentralized and transparent elections, financial inclusion	State-controlled blockchain to track and restrict financial transactions
Biometric Surveillance	Secure public spaces, improved accessibility, privacy-preserving identity management	Totalitarian surveillance, real-time citizen tracking, loss of anonymity
Quantum Computing	Unbreakable encryption securing privacy and democratic processes	Government-controlled quantum decryption undermining privacy and dissent
Neurotechnology	Cognitive freedom, enhanced learning, open-source brain-machine interfaces	Thought control, emotion regulation, and state-imposed cognitive manipulation
Synthetic Biology	Disease eradication, longevity, democratized access to bio-enhancements	Eugenics, state-controlled genetic modification, biopolitical hierarchies

AUTOMATION & ROBOTICS	Universal basic income, enhanced productivity, labor liberation	Mass unemployment, robotic policing, AI-led enforcement of state power
INTERNET OF THINGS (IOT)	Smart cities with participatory governance, real-time civic engagement	Pervasive data-driven social control, automated censorship, totalitarian command structures
AUGMENTED & VIRTUAL REALITY (AR/VR)	Immersive democratic forums, education and citizen engagement	Government-controlled virtual realities, propaganda, and digital escapism
5G & BEYOND	Equal access to high-speed information, global collaboration	Enhanced cyber warfare, increased state censorship, control over information flows
NANO-TECHNOLOGY	Disease prevention, environmental sustainability, abundance of resources	Ubiquitous micro-surveillance, nanobot-assisted state tracking
AUTONOMOUS WEAPONS	Ethical AI-driven deterrence, reduction of collateral damage in conflicts	AI-led warfare, automated military suppression of dissent
SATELLITE COMMUNICATION (E.G., STARLINK, ONEWEB, ETC.)	Universal internet access, bypassing state censorship, empowering remote and marginalized communities, decentralized information flow	State-controlled or corporate-dominated access, internet shutdowns, militarization of satellite networks, targeted disconnection of dissenting regions

Digital technology holds the potential to revitalize democracy by enabling participatory governance models where citizens have a direct role in decision-making. AI-assisted policymaking could help distribute resources fairly, while blockchain technology could secure voting systems from fraud. The decentralization of power through open-source platforms, digital town halls, and real-time civic engagement could create a more inclusive and accountable political system. However, digital technology is also being weaponized by extremist movements and authoritarian regimes to spread fascism online. The architecture of social media platforms is designed to prioritize engagement over truth, meaning that hate speech, conspiracy theories, and extremist ideologies are often amplified over more measured, fact-based discourse. This fosters a digital ecosystem where:

Algorithmic Radicalization: Right-wing authoritarianism spreads via recommendation algorithms, pulling users toward extremist content.

Echo Chambers & Filter Bubbles: Social media isolates individuals into ideological silos, reinforcing division and misinformation.

Mass Disinformation Campaigns: Governments and extremist groups exploit digital media to manipulate public perception and erode trust in democratic institutions.

Surveillance & Repression: AI-powered tracking and biometric databases enable authoritarian governments to preemptively identify and suppress dissent.

The battle between techno-democracy and techno-fascism is already underway. While digital technology can serve as a powerful force for political empowerment and democratic participation, it can also be used to automate oppression, manipulate public opinion, and spread authoritarian ideology. If we do not establish ethical frameworks, legal protections, and democratic oversight, digital tools will become the infrastructure of a high-tech dystopia. If we proactively shape technology for the public good, it can become a foundation for a more open, fair, and participatory society.

The 4th Industrial Revolution is not just about technology—it is about power. The choices we make today will determine whether AI, blockchain, and automation serve to empower individuals, protect privacy, and expand democratic participation or whether they become the infrastructure of a global surveillance state, algorithmic fascism, and digital totalitarianism. This is the defining political question of the digital age, one that will shape the future of governance, citizenship, and human freedom in ways we are only beginning to grasp. The unchecked power of digital oligarchs raises urgent concerns about democracy's survival—without robust regulation, social media platforms will continue amplifying authoritarian rhetoric, AI-driven surveillance will deepen systemic inequalities, and tech billionaires will consolidate their control over policymaking. Addressing these threats requires global cooperation, public awareness, and systemic reforms that prioritize democratic governance over algorithmic rule, ensuring that technology serves society rather than dominates it.

Technological Governance for Democratic Future

As techno-fascism gains traction, the central question becomes clear. How can democratic institutions push back against the encroachment of corporate technological power? Without proper regulatory frameworks, these technologies risk being exploited for private gain, undermining democratic institutions, and facilitating corrupt activities rather than serving the common good. Establishing robust and relevant regulatory frameworks is essential to counter the risks of techno-fascism and ensure that technological advancements align with democratic values. These frameworks should promote accountability, prevent corporate overreach, and safeguard fundamental rights. The following are key regulatory priorities that can help mitigate the concentration of technological power and uphold democratic governance:

1. Comprehensive Data Protection Law: Strong data privacy regulations, such as the European Union's General Data Protection Regulation (GDPR), should be expanded globally. Data protection laws must ensure transparency in data collection, grant users control over their personal information and enforce strict penalties for violations. The United States has debated federal privacy legislation, but a fragmented approach persists, with only state-level measures like the California Consumer Privacy Act (CCPA, 2018) offering some protections.

2. AI Governance and Ethical AI Development: Artificial intelligence must be developed and deployed within clear ethical and legal boundaries. The EU AI Act, for example, classifies AI applications by risk level, banning those that threaten fundamental rights. Similar frameworks should be adopted worldwide to prevent algorithmic bias, mass surveillance, and AI-driven decision-making that lacks human oversight (European Commission, 2024).

3. Antitrust and Competition Policy Reform: Big Tech monopolies wield disproportionate influence over information ecosystems and market competition. Strengthening antitrust regulations to prevent monopolistic practices by companies like Apple, Alphabet (Google), Amazon, Microsoft, and Meta (Facebook) is crucial. The American Innovation and Choice Online Act has been proposed to curb anti-competitive behavior, though enforcement remains a challenge due to corporate lobbying (Ingram, 2024).

4. Regulation of Digital Political Advertising and Disinformation: Tech platforms must be held accountable for the spread of disinformation and the manipulation of public opinion through opaque algorithmic processes. Governments should enforce transparency in political advertising and require social media companies to disclose funding sources and content moderation policies. The Digital Services Act (DSA) in the EU serves as a model for regulating online content and ensuring accountability for tech giants (European Commission, 2022).

5. Stronger Cybersecurity and Protection Against Digital Authoritarianism: Government leaders must develop cybersecurity policies that protect against state-backed digital warfare, cyberattacks, and mass surveillance. Initiatives like the United Nations Global Digital Compact (UNGDC) emphasize the need for international cooperation to safeguard the digital space from authoritarian control and cyber threats (United Nations, 2023).

6. International Cooperation on Digital Governance: Given the borderless nature of digital platforms, multilateral cooperation is essential for effective technology governance. Agreements like the Global Digital Compact and OECD principles on AI provide frameworks for ensuring that technological advancements respect human rights and democratic principles (OECD, 2019).

Beyond governmental intervention, citizen-led initiatives such as open-source movements, decentralized platforms, and algorithmic transparency advocacy offer alternative models for resisting algorithmic authoritarianism. Zeynep Tufekci (2017) in *Twitter and Tear Gas* examines how digital activism has been used to counteract state repression, demonstrating the power of collective action in resisting authoritarian digital control. Similarly, grassroots organizations advocating for AI ethics and responsible technology deployment emphasize the need for democratic oversight to prevent AI systems from exacerbating social inequalities (Pasquale, 2020).

Ethics and Education for Techno-Democracy

As a professor of ethical leadership practices in San Francisco—arguably the epicenter of the global techno-revolution—I see firsthand both the promise and the peril of our digital age. The breathtaking pace of innovation has outstripped the ethical frameworks meant to guide it. Regulation alone cannot safeguard democracy in a world increasingly governed by algorithms, artificial intelligence, and opaque data systems. What we need is a revolution in education—an intentional, values-driven approach that re-centers technology as a tool for inclusive development, social justice, and sustainable democratic governance.

Ethics and principled-value leadership must not be an afterthought — It must be the foundation of our professional and technically-intelligent education. We are witnessing a silent erosion of critical thinking—what I call the *civic imagination*—as over-reliance on AI-generated content numbs analytical reasoning and stifles our capacity to challenge, question, and co-create the world around us.

Research from institutions like Microsoft and MIT warns us that when intellectual agency is outsourced to machines, societies become easier to manipulate, less capable of civic discernment, and more vulnerable to digital authoritarianism (Gerlich, 2025). Maria Ressa (2022) captures this crisis with urgency. When people can no longer distinguish truth from disinformation, democracy begins to die. And make no mistake—this is not a hypothetical threat. It is already happening.

To reclaim technology for democracy, we must embed digital ethics and critical thinking into every layer of our education systems—from K–12 classrooms to university lecture halls, from professional training to public awareness campaigns. Citizens must understand how algorithms shape their realities, how media is engineered to polarize, and how power operates through code.

An informed, ethically grounded citizenry is the strongest defense against unchecked digital authoritarianism.

This is especially urgent in the United States, where legacy systems like the Electoral College amplify the voices of regions with limited access to digital literacy, leaving them more susceptible to misinformation and manipulation. Without an educational overhaul that democratizes access to digital fluency and ethical reasoning, we will continue to see our institutions destabilized by bad actors weaponizing technology for control.

The path forward demands a bold, unified strategy—grounded in strong regulation, transformative education, and ethical leadership. We must dismantle monopolistic power in the digital sphere and reimagine technology as a public good, serving the many, not the few. The choices we make today will determine whether future generations inherit thriving democracies that protect rights and dignity—or descend into digital authoritarianism that erodes our collective hopes for peace, justice, and well-being.

I feel the responsibility to help lead this transformation—not just by teaching how to use technology, but how to question it with courage, ethics, and critical insight. Leadership in this era is not about technical prowess alone; it's about moral clarity and a commitment to inclusive, sustainable progress.

The defining challenge of our time is not whether we *can* advance technology, but whether we *will* democratize it. The future of democracy hinges on what we teach, how we lead, and the ethical imagination we dare to cultivate—starting now.

EPILOGUE

Throughout this book, I've tried to answer one burning question: Why does fascism keep coming back? Why do seemingly decent people fall for dehumanizing ideologies that undermine dignity, truth, and democracy? And why, after all we've learned, do so many educational systems still treat these topics as relics of the past—something to memorize, not to truly understand?

Fascism is not just an event in the past. It is a mindset—a dangerous lens through which people are reduced to threats, dissent is equated with disloyalty, and fear becomes a political currency. As someone whose family lived through the devastations of World War II in Europe, I don't approach this subject abstractly. It lives in my blood. I was born just a generation removed from the wreckage of fascist violence, and I grew up hearing stories that shaped my sense of responsibility—not only as a citizen but as an educator and a human being.

One of the key inspirations for this book comes from a conversation I had many years ago in Florence with Prof. Chiavacci, a wise and principled educator who spoke often of *subsidiarietà*—the idea that decision-making power should reside as close as possible to the people it affects. He believed, as I do, that education must be a force for liberation, not indoctrination. That our responsibility as teachers is not to feed students answers, but to train them to question, discern, and think critically. He taught me that democracy cannot be preserved without subsidiarity. That lesson has stayed with me ever since.

And it's never been more relevant. We live in an age where disinformation is algorithmically amplified, where technologies built to connect are weaponized to divide, and where democratic institutions are being hollowed out in real time. Without the ability to distinguish truth from propaganda, sincere leadership from performative populism, we risk losing everything generations before us fought to protect.

The Italian proverb that opened this book—*Fare di tutta l'erba un fascio*—warns us against lumping everything together without discernment. But that is exactly what is happening. People confuse public health measures with tyranny, civic responsibility with oppression, regulation with coercion. That failure to tell the difference isn't harmless—it is the very gateway through which fascism re-enters the cultural bloodstream.

Discernment, then, is not an option in our lives or just an elective in our curriculum. It is a civic duty and a global citizenship responsibility. As Sfeir-Younis (2021) has written, the path to ethical leadership begins with multilateral consciousness—a disciplined effort to see clearly and act justly. Discernment is therefore the essential pathway for conscious leadership for the common good (Sfeir-Younis & Tavanti, 2020; Tavanti & Wilp, 2021).

True leadership requires knowing the difference between power that protects and power that manipulates. It demands choosing the common good over personal gain. As Nelson Mandela put it, "What counts in life is not the mere fact that we have lived. It is what difference we have made to the lives of others" (Mandela, 2003). The contrast between ego-fascist leadership and common good-conscious leadership is not merely theoretical—it is a decisive factor shaping societies, economies, and the future of humanity itself. Ego-fascist leadership thrives on fear, division, and the consolidation of power in the hands of a few. It favors control over collaboration, obedience over empowerment, and short-term personal gain over long-term collective well-being (Tavanti, 2024). History has shown that such leadership—rooted in manipulation, exclusion, and centralized authority—inevitably leads to oppression, systemic inequality, and societal instability

I've written this book as both a (critical) scholar and a (global) citizen—as someone who has spent decades studying leadership systems, ethics, and sustainability, but also as someone who has watched the world teeter toward chaos too many times. It is both an analytical guide and a deeply personal reflection. The comparative tools and leadership tables are meant to help you think, not just memorize. To help you see the difference between leaders who build and those who exploit, between governance and control, between responsibility and dominance.

We are standing at a crossroads. Down one path lies **neo-corporatist authoritarianism**—a future where governments and corporations merge to create systems of total control, where AI surveillance, predictive analytics, and biometric data govern our lives with little transparency. On the other path is a still-emerging **decentralized technological democracy**—a world where open-source tools, civic participation, and ethical innovation keep power in the hands of people, not platforms.

What we choose now matters. If you have the privilege to vote, to teach, to create, to lead, to speak—you have a duty. A duty to resist disinformation, to reject apathy, and to actively build systems that prioritize sustainability, justice, and collective well-being. Educators must guard classrooms as sanctuaries of inquiry. Business leaders must redefine success to include impact and equity. Citizens must never surrender their agency, no matter how loud or sophisticated the propaganda becomes.

And we must never forget that we are not the first to face this challenge. On May 8, 1945, when Nazi Germany surrendered, the delegates at the San Francisco Conference (UNCIO, United Nations Conference for International Organization) were still gathered—crafting the United Nations Charter with trembling hope for a peaceful future. The words they inscribed in its Preamble remain a living call to conscience and responsibility:

> We the peoples of the United Nations determined to save succeeding generations from the scourge of war, which twice in our lifetime has brought untold sorrow to mankind, and to reaffirm faith in fundamental human rights, in the dignity and worth of the human person, in the equal rights of men and women and of nations large and small, and to establish conditions under which justice and respect for the obligations arising from treaties and other sources of international law can be maintained, and to promote social progress and better standards of life in larger freedom (United Nations, 1945).

Just eleven days later, on May 19, they gathered beneath the redwoods of Muir Woods National Monument to honor the legacy of President Franklin D. Roosevelt—who had envisioned that global gathering but did not live to see its completion. The towering trees of Cathedral Grove, once endangered by exploitation, became a monument to human cooperation and a reminder that even the most fragile hopes can be preserved through collective will.

Barack Obama reminded us of our personal and collective leadership responsibility when he said this at the 2014 U.N. Climate Summit, *"We are the first generation to fully grasp [the climate crisis]—and the last with the chance to take decisive action"* (Obama, 2014). That truth applies to many crises we face not just environmental collapse, but also the erosion of democracy, the rise of algorithmic manipulation, and the moral void at the heart of modern leadership.

And sometimes, doing the right thing means disrupting the norm. It means pushing back against what Congressman **John Lewis** so powerfully called *"good trouble"*—the kind of necessary disruption that interrupts injustice, challenges the status quo, and refuses to accept business as usual when business as usual is unethical. He taught us that nonviolent resistance is not the opposite of leadership—it is its most courageous expression. Good trouble happens when marginalized voices are ignored, when laws serve the powerful rather than the people, and when silence becomes complicity. It's the spark that keeps moral leadership alive.

I've always believed that leadership must be grounded in something deeper than strategy or style—it must be rooted in a sense of shared humanity. I often return to this idea when I teach. In one of my leadership lectures, I show my students a photo of General Dwight D. Eisenhower taken just before the D-Day invasion. Amid all the pressure, all the decisions, all the weight of history on his shoulders, he walked among the soldiers of the 101st Airborne Division. He looked them in the eye. He knew many would not come back. That moment reminds me that leadership—real leadership—is about human connection, about bearing responsibility for others with clarity and compassion.

That same principle was reaffirmed in 1948 with the adoption of the Universal Declaration of Human Rights (UDHR), a visionary document shaped by Eleanor Roosevelt and enriched by other women leaders who had participated in the UNCIO Conference. It remains one of the most inspiring affirmations of our shared dignity—a milestone in the ongoing journey toward global justice.

And more recently, I was reminded again—quietly, unexpectedly—on a visit to the Imperial War Museum in London. In the World War II exhibit, I saw a small medal awarded to a young French resistance fighter. It bore an inscription from the Talmud:

"Whoever saves one life saves the entire world."

That line pierced through everything. Because in the end, this isn't just about ideologies or institutions. It's about people. It's about the choices we make every day—what we vote for, what we teach, what we tolerate, what we resist. Leadership begins not with titles or roles, but with the simple, often unseen decisions we make to protect what matters.

Each of us has the capacity to make a difference—sometimes quietly, sometimes boldly, sometimes by getting into a little good trouble.

This book is my contribution to that effort.

A tool for decoding the complexities of leadership today. A tribute to those who came before. A guide for those preparing to lead tomorrow.

And a reminder that when the stakes are high, resistance is not just justified—it is necessary.

Don't just memorize—galvanize.
Lead with conscience.
Protect what matters.
And when justice demands it, get into good trouble.
May this book inspire your courage—and your action.

REFERENCES

Acemoglu, D., & Johnson, S. (2023). Power and progress: Our thousand-year struggle over technology and prosperity. *PublicAffairs*.

Acemoglu, D., & Robinson, J. A. (2006). *Economic origins of dictatorship and democracy*. Cambridge University Press.

Acemoglu, D., & Robinson, J. A. (2012). *Why nations fail: The origins of power, prosperity, and poverty*. Crown Business.

Acemoglu, D., & Robinson, J. A. (2019). *The narrow corridor: States, societies, and the fate of liberty*. Penguin Press.

Acton, J. E. E. (1887). Letter to Bishop Creighton.

Agocs, A. (2017). *Antifascist humanism and the politics of cultural renewal in Germany*. Cambridge University Press.

Alexander, D. (1984). The reclamation of Val-di-Chiana (Tuscany). *Annals of the Association of American Geographers, 74*(4), 527-550. https://doi.org/10.1111/j.1467-8306.1984.tb01472.x

Ambrose, S. E. (1992). *Band of brothers: E Company, 506th Regiment, 101st Airborne from Normandy to Hitler's Eagle's Nest*. Simon & Schuster.

Anderson, J. Q., & Rainie, L. (2020). Concerns about democracy in the digital age. *Pew Research Center*. February 21. https://www.pewresearch.org/internet/2020/02/21/concerns-about-democracy-in-the-digital-age/

Apple, M. W. (2021). *Knowledge, power, and education: The selected works of Michael W. Apple*. Routledge.

Arendt, H. (2006). *Eichmann in Jerusalem: A report on the banality of evil* (Rev. ed.). Penguin Classics. (Original work published 1963)

Arjomand, S. A. (2019). *The political dimensions of religion: Theocracy and clericalism in the modern world*. Oxford University Press.

Atkinson, R. (2002). *An army at dawn: The war in North Africa, 1942-1943*. Henry Holt & Co.

Badgett, M. V. (2020). *The economic case for LGBT equality: Why fair and equal treatment benefits us all.* Beacon Press.

Baldini, M., & Cavallaro, G. (2010). *Stragi nazifasciste in Toscana: Civitella e la memoria divisa.* Laterza.

Baranowski, S., Nolzen, A., & Szejnmann, C. C. W. (Eds.). (2018). *A companion to Nazi Germany.* John Wiley & Sons.

Bass, B. M. (1990). *Handbook of leadership: Theory, research, and managerial applications* (3rd ed.). Free Press.

Battini, M. (2014). *Peccati di memoria: La mancata Norimberga italiana.* Laterza.

BBC (2013). *In quotes: Italy's Silvio Berlusconi in his own words.* https://www.bbc.com/news/world-europe-15642201

Bello, W. F. (2019). *Counterrevolution: The Global Rise of the Far Right.* Fernwood Publishing.

Bello, W. F. (2024, July 9). How to Counter Fascism: Fascism is not inevitable. Not if we put ourselves, body and soul, fully and smartly, on the line to stop it. *Foreign Policy in Focus (FPIF)* https://fpif.org/how-to-counter-fascism/

Ben-Ghiat, R. (2020). *Strongmen: Mussolini to the present.* W. W. Norton & Company.

Benkler, Y. (2006). *The wealth of networks: How social production transforms markets and freedom.* Yale University Press.

Bennett, D. H. (2018). *The party of fear: From nativist movements to the New Right in American history.* UNC Press.

Bennis, W. (1989). *On becoming a leader.* Addison-Wesley.

Bezio, K. M., & Goethals, G. R. (Eds.). (2020). *Leadership, Populism, and Resistance.* Edward Elgar Publishing.

Blamires, C., & Jackson, P. (2006). *World Fascism: A Historical Encyclopedia.* ABC-CLIO.

Blau, J. (2017). The paradox of American exceptionalism. In *The Paris Agreement: Climate Change, Solidarity, and Human Rights* (pp. 45-56). Springer.

Bloom, P. (2016). *Beyond Power and Resistance: Politics at the Radical Limits.* Rowman & Littlefield International.

Bogdanor, V. (1995). *The monarchy and the constitution.* Oxford University Press.

Bonhoeffer, D. (n.d.). Attributed quote on moral society.

Börzel, T. A., Risse, T., Anderson, S. B., & Garrison, J. A. (Eds.). (2024). *Polarization and deep contestations: The liberal script in the United States.* Oxford University Press.

Bosworth, R. J. B. (2006). *Mussolini's Italy: Life under the Fascist Dictatorship, 1915-1945.* Penguin Books.

Bowman, J. S., & West, J. P. (2021). *Public service ethics: Individual and institutional responsibilities.* Routledge.

Bray, M. (2017). *Antifa: The anti-fascist handbook.* Melville House.

Braskén, K., Copsey, N., & Featherstone, D. J. (Eds.). (2020). *Anti-fascism in a global perspective: Transnational networks, exile communities, and radical internationalism.* Routledge.

Brin, D. (1998). *The transparent society: Will technology force us to choose between privacy and freedom?* Perseus Books.

Brito, J., & Castillo, A. (2023). *Blockchain governance: Balancing innovation and regulation.* MIT Press.

Brown, A. (1996). *The Gorbachev factor.* Oxford University Press.

Burns, J. M. (1978). *Leadership.* Harper & Row.

California Consumer Privacy Act (CCPA). (2018, October 15). State of California - Department of Justice - Office of the Attorney General. https://oag.ca.gov/privacy/ccpa

Camayd-Freixas, E. (2008). Teaching Liberation Theology: The Legacy of Las Casas. Approaches to Teaching the Writings of Bartolomé de las Casas. In Arias, S. and Merediz E.M. Eds). *Approaches to Teaching the Writings of Bartolomé de Las Casas* (pp. 187-195). Modern Language Association of America.

Camus, R. (2018). *You Will Not Replace Us!* Chez l'auteur.

Carlyle, T. (1841). *On heroes, hero-worship, and the heroic in history.* James Fraser.

Cerise, L. (2023). *Governing by Chaos: Social Engineering and Globalization - Essais – Documents.* Max Milo.

Chafkin, M. (2021). *The Contrarian: Peter Thiel and Silicon Valley's Pursuit of Power.* Bloomsbury Publishing.

Chayka, K. (2025, February 26). Elon Musk, and How Techno-Fascism Has Come to America. *The New Yorker.* https://www.newyorker.com/culture/infinite-scroll/techno-fascism-comes-to-america-elon-musk

Chiavacci, E. (2001). *Lezioni brevi di etica sociale.* Cittadella Editrice.

Chomsky, N. (2010, April 10). Interview with Chris Hedges. *Truthdig.* https://www.truthdig.com/

Churchill, W. (1947, November 11). Speech before the House of Commons. Hansard, HC Deb, 444, cc206–07. Retrieved from https://api.parliament.uk/historic-hansard/commons/1947/nov/11/parliament-bill#column_206

Ciulla, J. B. (2004). *Ethics, the heart of leadership.* Praeger.

Cohen, D. & Mikaelian, A. (2021). *The Privatization of Everything: How the Plunder of Public Goods Transformed America and How We Can Fight Back.* New Press.

Collier, P. (2018). *The future of capitalism: Facing the new anxieties.* Harper.

Collingwood, R. G. (1946). *The idea of history.* Clarendon Press.

Critical Race Theory (CRT), 126, 128

Dahl, R. A. (2006). *On Democracy.* Yale University Press.

Dahl, R. A. (2008). *On Political Equality.* Yale University Press.

Dalton, R. J. (2012). *The Apartisan American: Dealignment and changing electoral politics.* CQ Press.

Darity, W. A. (2008). *International encyclopedia of the social sciences.* Macmillan.

Davies, J., & Davies, D. (2010). "Origins and evolution of antibiotic resistance." Microbiology and molecular biology reviews, 74(3), 417-433.

De Felice, R. (1995). *Interpretations of fascism.* Harvard University Press.

Delgado, R., & Stefancic, J. (2017). *Critical race theory: An introduction* (3rd ed.). NYU Press.

Denhardt, R. B., & Denhardt, J. V. (2000). The new public service: Serving rather than steering. *Public Administration Review,* 60(6), 549-559.

Derbyshire, J. D., & Derbyshire, I. (2016). *Encyclopedia of World Political Systems.* Routledge.

Diamond, L. (2019). *Ill Winds: Saving democracy from Russian rage, Chinese ambition, and American complacency.* Penguin Press.

DiResta, R. (2024). *Invisible Rulers: The People Who Turn Lies Into Reality.* PublicAffairs.

Diversity, Equity and Inclusion (DEI), 124, 124

Eatwell, R. (2011). *Fascism: A History.* Random House.

Eatwell, R. (2017). *National populism: The revolt against liberal democracy.* Pelican Books.
Esmark, A. (2020). *The New Technocracy.* Bristol University Press.
Eubanks, V. (2018). *Automating inequality: How high-tech tools profile, police, and punish the poor.* St. Martin's Press.
European Commission. (2022). *The EU's Digital Services Act (DSA).* https://commission.europa.eu/strategy-and-policy/priorities-2019-2024/europe-fit-digital-age/digital-services-act_en
European Commission. (2024). *EU AI Act: Regulatory framework on artificial intelligence.* https://artificialintelligenceact.eu/
Fattorini, E. (2011). *Hitler, Mussolini and the Vatican: Pope Pius XI and the Speech That was Never Made.* Polity Press.
Feldstein, S. (2021). *The Rise of Digital Repression: How Technology is Reshaping Power, Politics, and Resistance.* Oxford University Press.
Fiedler, F. E. (1967). *A theory of leadership effectiveness.* McGraw-Hill.
Filippi, F. (2020). *Ma perché siamo ancora fascisti? Un conto rimasto aperto* [Why are we still fascists? An open account]. Bollati Boringhieri.
Finchelstein, F. (2022). *A Brief History of Fascist Lies.* University of California Press.
Finchelstein, F. (2024). *The Wannabe Fascists: A Guide to Understanding the Greatest Threat to Democracy.* University of California Press.
Finer, S. E. (2017). *The history of government from the earliest times.* Oxford University Press.
Fischer, F. (1990). *Technocracy and the politics of expertise.* SAGE Publications.
Foot, J. (2022). *Blood and Power: The Rise and Fall of Italian Fascism.* United Kingdom: Bloomsbury Publishing.
Forgacs, D. (Ed.). (2000). *The Antonio Gramsci Reader: Selected Writings 1916–1935.* NYU Press.
Francis, P. (2015). *Laudato Si': On care for our common home.* Vatican Press.
Freire, P. (1970). *Pedagogy of the oppressed.* Bloomsbury Academic.
Freire, P. (2000). *Education for critical consciousness.* Continuum.
Friedman, J. (2019). *Power Without Knowledge: A Critique of Technocracy.* Oxford University Press.
Fuchs, C. (2022). *Digital Fascism: Media, Communication and Society Volume Four.* Taylor & Francis.

Fukuyama, F. (2011). *The origins of political order: From prehuman times to the French Revolution.* Farrar, Straus and Giroux.

Fukuyama, F. (2014). *Political order and political decay: From the industrial revolution to the globalization of democracy.* Farrar, Straus and Giroux.

Gadotti, M. (1994). *Reading Paulo Freire: His life and work.* State University of New York Press.

Gallo, E. (2022). Three varieties of authoritarian neoliberalism: Rule by the experts, the people, the leader. *Competition & Change, 26*(5), 554-574.

Gandhi, M. (1995). *The collected works of Mahatma Gandhi (Vol. 15).* Publications Division, Government of India. (Original work published 1913)

Gandhi, M. (n.d.). Attributed quote on social justice and vulnerability.

Gardner, H. (1983). *Frames of mind: The theory of multiple intelligences.* Basic Books.

Gentile, E. (1996). *The sacralization of politics in fascist Italy.* Harvard University Press.

Gentile, E. (2005a). *The origins of fascist ideology: 1918-1925.* Enigma Books.

Gentile, E. (2005b). *Fascismo: Storia e interpretazione.* Laterza.

Gerlich, M. (2025). AI Tools in Society: Impacts on Cognitive Offloading and the Future of Critical Thinking. *Societies, 15*(1), 6. https://doi.org/10.3390/soc15010006

Gessen, M. (2025, March 17). Opinion | There's a name for what Trump is doing to trans people: Denationalizing. *The New York Times.* https://www.nytimes.com/2025/03/17/opinion/trump-trans-denationalizing.html

Gilbert, L., & Mohseni, P. (2011). Beyond authoritarianism: The conceptualization of hybrid regimes. *Studies in Comparative International Development, 46*(3), 270–297.

Gilbert, M. (2024). *Italy Reborn: From Fascism to Democracy.* Random House.

Giroux, H. A. (2018). *American nightmare: Facing the challenge of fascism.* City Lights Books.

Goldstein, D., & Gutkin, L. (2025, March 12). We're in the Midst of an Authoritarian Takeover. *The Chronicle of Higher Education.* https://www.chronicle.com/article/were-in-the-midst-of-an-authoritarian-takeover

Goleman, D. (1995). *Emotional intelligence: Why it can matter more than IQ.* Bantam Books.

Gorski, P. S., & Perry, S. L. (2022). *The Flag and the Cross: White Christian Nationalism and the Threat to American Democracy.* Oxford University Press.

Graeber, D. (2013). *The democracy project: A history, a crisis, a movement.* Spiegel & Grau.

Gramsci, A. (1971). *Selections from the prison notebooks.* International Publishers.

Gramsci, A. (2000). *The Antonio Gramsci Reader: Selected Writings 1916-1935.* NYU Press.

Greenleaf, R. K. (1977). *Servant leadership: A journey into the nature of legitimate power and greatness.* Paulist Press.

Gregor, A. J. (2005). *The ideology of fascism: The rationale of totalitarianism.* Free Press.

Gurr, T. R. (1970). *Why Men Rebel.* Princeton University Press.

Habermas, J. (1992). *Between Facts and Norms: Contributions to a Discourse Theory of Law and Democracy.* MIT Press.

Habermas, J. (2023). *A new structural transformation of the public sphere and deliberative politics.* Polity Press.

Harari, Y. N. (2018). *21 lessons for the 21st century.* Spiegel & Grau.

Harvey, N. (1998). *The Chiapas rebellion: The struggle for land and democracy.* Duke University Press.

Hebblethwaite, P. (1993). *Paul VI: The first modern pope.* HarperCollins.

Hegel, G. W. F. (1956). *The philosophy of history* (J. Sibree, Trans.). Dover Publications. (Original work published 1837).

Heifetz, R. A. (1994). *Leadership without easy answers.* Harvard University Press.

Hein, L. (2018). *Post-Fascist Japan: Political Culture in Kamakura After the Second World War.* Bloomsbury Publishing.

Hemingway, E. (1940). *For whom the bell tolls.* Charles Scribner's Sons.

Hersey, P., & Blanchard, K. H. (1969). *Management of organizational behavior: Utilizing human resources.* Prentice-Hall.

Heywood, A. (2021). *Politics.* Palgrave Macmillan.

Hillman, J. E. (2022). *Techno-Authoritarianism: Platform for Repression in China and Abroad.* Center for Strategic and International Studies (CSIS).

Huntington, S. P. (1991). *The third wave: Democratization in the late twentieth century.* University of Oklahoma Press.

Huntington, S. P. (2004). *Who are we? The challenges to America's national identity.* Simon & Schuster.

Ingram, J. H. (2024). Transforming Antitrust Laws: Lawmakers Attempt to "Fix" Competition by Targeting Big Tech. *Cumberland Law Review,* 54, 431.

Jacobsson, S., & Bergek, A. (2004). Transforming the energy sector: The evolution of technological systems in renewable energy technology. *Industrial and Corporate Change,* 13(5), 815-849.

Kagan, R. (2024). *Rebellion: How Antiliberalism Is Tearing America Apart-Again.* Knopf Doubleday Publishing Group.

Kallis, A. (2000). *Fascist ideology: Territory and expansionism in Italy and Germany, 1922-1945.* Routledge.

Kennedy, J. F. (1963). *Commencement address at Vanderbilt University.* U.S. Government Printing Office.

Keohane, R. O. (2020). *After hegemony: Cooperation and discord in the world political economy (2nd ed.).* Princeton University Press.

Kershaw, I. (1998). *Hitler: 1889-1936 Hubris.* W.W. Norton & Company.

Kersten, R. (2013). *Democracy in post-war Japan: Maruyama Masao and the search for autonomy.* Routledge.

Klinkhammer, L. (1993). *Stragi naziste in Italia: La guerra contro i civili (1943-1945).* Donzelli.

Kurtz, L. R. (2020). *Encyclopedia of Violence, Peace, and Conflict.* Elsevier.

Lao Tzu. (1972). *Tao Te Ching* (G. Feng & J. English, Trans.). Vintage Books.

Lennick, D., & Kiel, F. (2005). *Moral intelligence: Enhancing business performance and leadership success.* Wharton School Publishing.

Levitsky, S., & Way, L. A. (2020). *Competitive authoritarianism: Hybrid regimes after the Cold War.* Cambridge University Press.

Levitsky, S., & Ziblatt, D. (2018). *How democracies die.* Crown Publishing.

Levitsky, S., Ziblatt, D. (2023). *Tyranny of the Minority: Why American Democracy Reached the Breaking Point.* Crown.

Lewandowsky, S. (2025). Free speech, fact checking, and the right to accurate information. *Science,* 387(6734).

Lincoln, A. (1854). Speech in Peoria, Illinois.

Linz, J. J. (2000). *Totalitarian and authoritarian regimes*. Lynne Rienner Publishers.

Lyons, O. (1980). *The wisdom of the elders: A conversation with Oren Lyons*. The Harvard Project on American Indian Economic Development.

Machiavelli, N. (1998). *Discourses on Livy* (H. C. Mansfield & N. Tarcov, Trans.). University of Chicago Press. (Original work published 1531).

Machiavelli, N. (2003). *The Prince* (P. Bondanella, Trans.). Oxford University Press. (Original work published 1532).

Maddow, R. (2023). Prequel: An American fight against fascism. Crown.

Madison, J. (1788). *The Federalist Papers*. No. 47. Retrieved from https://www.congress.gov/resources/display/content/The+Federalist+Papers

Mandela, N. (2003). Speech delivered on July 1, 2003, at the launch of the Nelson Mandela Foundation in Johannesburg, South Africa.

Marcus, R. (2018, January 20). Trump said: 'I alone can fix it.' How wrong he was. *The Washington Post*.

Marshall, M. G., & Gurr, T. R. (2020). *Polity IV dataset: Political regime characteristics and transitions, 1800-2018*. Center for Systemic Peace.

Marshall, P. (2009). *Demanding the impossible: A history of anarchism*. PM Press.

Martin, W. (2005). *With God on Our Side: The Rise of the Religious Right in America*. Broadway Books.

Marx, K. (1852/2008). The eighteenth Brumaire of Louis Bonaparte (D. De Leon, Trans.). *International Publishers*. (Original work published 1852)

Marx, K. (1992). *Capital: A critique of political economy, Volume 1* (B. Fowkes, Trans.). Penguin Classics. (Original work published 1867).

Mason, P. (2021). *How To Stop Fascism: History, Ideology, Resistance*. Allen Lane.

Mazzucato, M. (2018). *The value of everything: Making and taking in the global economy*. PublicAffairs.

McAdam, D., Tarrow, S., & Tilly, C. (2001). *Dynamics of Contention*. Cambridge University Press.

McDonnell, D., & Valbruzzi, M. (2014). Defining and classifying technocratic governments. *European Journal of Political Research, 53*(4), 654–671.

McLaren, P. (2022). Critical pedagogy: A look at the major concepts. In *Critical pedagogy and globalization* (pp. 13–30). Routledge.

Milani, L. (1967). *Lettera a una professoressa* (Letter to a teacher). Libreria Editrice Fiorentina.

Milani, l. (1971), *Lettera ai Giudici* (Letter to the Judges), in *L'obbedienza non é più una virtù* (Obedience is no longer a virtue) (pp. 29-62), Libreria Editrice Fiorentina.

Milani, L. (2008). *L'obbedienza non è più una virtù: Testi e lettere*. Libreria Editrice Fiorentina.

Milani, L. & Barbiana School (2004). *Letter to a teacher* (N. Alessandrini, Trans.). New York Review of Books. (Original work published 1967)

Mimura, J. (2011). *Planning for empire: Reform bureaucrats and the Japanese wartime state*. Cornell University Press.

Montesquieu, C. (1748). *The Spirit of the Laws*. Cambridge University Press.

Morozov, E. (2013). *To save everything, click here: The folly of technological solutionism*. PublicAffairs.

Mounk, Y. (2022). *The great experiment: Why diverse democracies fall apart and how they can endure*. Penguin Press.

Mounk, Y. (2022). *The People vs. Democracy: Why Our Freedom Is in Danger and How to Save It*. Harvard University Press.

Mozur, P. (2018, October 15). A genocide incited on Facebook, with posts from Myanmar's military. *The New York Times*. https://www.nytimes.com/2018/10/15/technology/myanmar-facebook-genocide.html

Mudde, C., & Rovira Kaltwasser, C. (2017). *Populism: A very short introduction*. Oxford University Press.

Murthy, V., & McKie, D. (2008). Learning from historical periods: zeitgeist correlations between environment, leadership, and strategy. *World Review of Entrepreneurship, Management and Sustainable Development*, 4(4), 331-344.

Mussolini, B. (1927). Make America great [Video]. *Internet Archive*. https://archive.org/details/benito-mussolini-make-america-great-1927

Mussolini, B. (1933). *The doctrine of fascism*. Vallecchi Editore.

Naím, M. (2022). *The Revenge of Power: How Autocrats Are Reinventing Politics for the 21st Century*. St. Martin's Publishing Group.

Nordlinger, E. A. (2009). *Soldiers in politics: Military coups and governments*. Princeton University Press.

Norris, P., & Inglehart, R. (2019). *Cultural backlash: Trump, Brexit, and authoritarian populism.* Cambridge University Press.

North, D. C. (1990). *Institutions, institutional change, and economic performance.* Cambridge University Press.

Northouse, P. G. (2021). *Leadership: Theory and practice* (9th ed.). Sage.

Obama, B. (2014, September 23). Remarks by the President at U.N. Climate Change Summit. Whitehouse.gov; Whitehouse. https://obamawhitehouse.archives.gov/the-press-office/2014/09/23/remarks-president-un-climate-change-summit

OECD. (2019). OECD principles on artificial intelligence. https://www.oecd.org

Orwell, G. (1949). *Nineteen Eighty-Four.* Secker & Warburg.

O'Donnell, G. (2019). *Modernization and bureaucratic-authoritarianism: Studies in South American politics.* University of California Press.

O'Donnell, J. (2020). *Democracy in Exile: Hans Speier and the Rise of the Defense Intellectual.* Princeton University Press.

O'Neil, C. (2016). *Weapons of math destruction: How big data increases inequality and threatens democracy.* Crown Publishing Group.

Pasolini, P. P. (1975). *Scritti corsari.* Garzanti.

Pasquale, F. (2020). *New laws of robotics: Defending human expertise in the age of AI.* Harvard University Press.

Paxton, R. O. (2005). *The anatomy of fascism.* Knopf.

Pellegrini, L. (2008). *Il catasto di Angiolo Tavanti e le riforme del Granducato di Toscana.* Firenze University Press.

Perrin, D. B., (2015). *Archbishop Romero and Spiritual Leadership in the Modern World.* Lexington Books..

Pertini, S. (1973). *Discorsi parlamentari.* Camera dei Deputati.

Plato. (2004). *The Republic* (ca. 375 BCE; C. D. C. Reeve, Trans.). Hackett Publishing.

Pollard, J. (1998). *The Fascist Experience in Italy.* Routledge.

Pollard, J. (2011). Fascism and Religion. In: Pinto, A.C. (eds) *Rethinking the Nature of Fascism.* Palgrave Macmillan, London. https://doi.org/10.1057/9780230295001_6

Polman, P. (2014). Business, society, and the future of capitalism. *McKinsey Quarterly, 1* (May).

Pritzker, JB (2025). Illinois Governor commenting on a month into President Donald Trump's second term in the White House. In Meisel, H. (2025, February 25). Pritzker positions himself at forefront of Trump opposition by invoking Nazis' rise to power. *Capitol News Illinois.* https://capitolnewsillinois.com/news/pritzker-positions-himself-at-forefront-of-trump-opposition-by-invoking-nazis-rise-to-power/

Pugliese, S. G. (Ed.). (2004). *Fascism, Anti-fascism, and the Resistance in Italy: 1919 to the Present.* Rowman & Littlefield Publishers.

Putnam, R. D. (1973). *The belief gap: A study of attitudes toward democracy and socialism in the Soviet Union.* Yale University Press.

Rachman, G. (2021). *The age of the strongman: How the cult of the leader threatens democracy around the world.* Other Press.

Rawls, J. (1971). *A theory of justice.* Harvard University Press.

Reagan, R. (1981). Inaugural Address.

Ressa, M. (2022). *How to stand up to a dictator: The fight for our future.* HarperCollins.

Rhodes, J. (2007). *Framing the Black Panthers: The spectacular rise of a Black power icon.* University of Illinois Press.

Roberts, A. (2014). *Napoleon: A life.* Penguin.

Rodríguez-Pose, A. (2020). The Rise of Populism and the Revenge of the Places That Don't Matter. *LSE Public Policy Review, 1*(1). https://doi.org/10.31389/lseppr.4

Roosevelt, F. D. (1938). *State of the Union Address.* U.S. Government Printing Office.

Roosevelt, F. D. (1945). *Address to the Congress on the Yalta Conference.* U.S. Government Printing Office.

Roosevelt, T. (1918). *The Great Adventure: present-day studies in American nationalism.* C. Scribner's Sons.

Sachs, J. D., Thwaites, J., Koundouri, P., & Sachs, L. (2022). Transforming multilateral development banks for climate finance. *Nature Sustainability,* 5(6), 453-460. https://doi.org/10.xxxx/natsustain12345

Schaake, M. (2024). *The Tech Coup: How to Save Democracy from Silicon Valley.* Princeton University Press.

Schmitter, P. C. (2020). *Still the century of corporatism? Revisiting state-corporate relationships.* Cambridge University Press.

Scott, J. C. (2012). *Two cheers for anarchism: Six easy pieces on autonomy, dignity, and meaningful work and play*. Princeton University Press.

Scurati, A. (2022). M: Son of the Century: A Novel. United Kingdom: HarperCollins.

Sen, A. (2017). *Ethics and economics*. Oxford University Press.

Sfeir-Younis, A. (2021, October 10). Preventing The Collapse of Multilateralism: Towards a Values-Based Planetary Governance. *Medium*. https://medium.com/@planethealingpress/preventing-the-collapse-of-multilateralism-towards-a-value-based-planetary-governance-e75550dac603

Sfeir-Younis, A. & Tavanti, M. (2020). *Conscious Sustainability Leadership: A New Paradigm for Next Generation Leaders*. Planet Healing Press.

Sieber-Gasser, C., & Ghibellini, A. (Eds.). (2021). *Democracy and globalization: Legal and political analysis on the eve of the 4th industrial revolution (Vol. 10)*. Springer Nature.

Sinek, S. (2014). *Leaders eat last: Why some teams pull together and others don't*. Portfolio.

Skinner, Q. (1978). *The foundations of modern political thought, Vol. 1: The Renaissance*. Cambridge University Press.

Smith, A. (1976). *An inquiry into the nature and causes of the wealth of nations*. University of Chicago Press. (Original work published 1776)

Smith, A. (2002). *The theory of moral sentiments*. Cambridge University Press. (Original work published 1759)

Snow, D. A., & Benford, R. D. (1988). "Ideology, Frame Resonance, and Participant Mobilization." *International Social Movement Research*, 1, 197-217.

Soni, J. (2022). *The Founders: The Story of Paypal and the Entrepreneurs Who Shaped Silicon Valley*. Simon & Schuster.

Spencer, H. (1896). *The study of sociology*. Appleton.

Stahel, W. R. (2016). The circular economy. *Nature*, 531(7595), 435-438.

Stanley, J. (2018). *How fascism works: The politics of us and them*. Random House.

Stanley, J. (2024). *Erasing History: How Fascists Rewrite the Past to Control the Future*. Footnote Press Limited.

Steinmetz-Jenkins, D. (Ed.). (2024). *Did it happen here?: perspectives on fascism and America*. WW Norton & Company.

Stern, S. J. (2004). *Remembering Pinochet's Chile: On the Eve of London 1998.* Duke University Press.

Stiglitz, J. E. (2010). *Freefall: America, free markets, and the sinking of the world economy.* W.W. Norton & Company.

Sugrue, T. (2008). *Sweet land of liberty: The forgotten struggle for civil rights in the North.* Random House.

Syme, R. (1939). *The Roman revolution.* Oxford University Press.

Tarrow, S. G. (2011). *Power in Movement: Social Movements and Contentious Politics.* Cambridge University Press.

Tavanti, M. & Stachowicz-Stanusch, A. (2014). *Sustainable Human Security: Corruption Issues and Anti-corruption Solutions.* Common Grounds Publishing.

Tavanti, M., & Wilp, A. E. (2021). A Common Good Mindset: An Integrated Model for Sustainability and Leadership Management Education. In I. Rimanoczy & A. Ritz (Eds.), *Sustainability Mindset and Transformative Leadership: A Multidisciplinary Perspective* (pp. 241-266). Palgrave Macmillan.

Tavanti, M. (2003). *Las Abejas: Pacifist resistance and syncretic identities in a globalizing Chiapas.* Routledge.

Tavanti, M. (2012). The cultural dimensions of Italian leadership: Power distance, uncertainty avoidance and masculinity from an American perspective. *Leadership,* 8(3), 287–301.

Tavanti, M. (2022). Ethics-Cases. Nonprofit Leadership Blog at the University of San Francisco's School of Management. https://usfblogs.usfca.edu/nonprofit/ethics/

Tavanti, M. (2023). *Sustainability Ethics: Common Good Values for a Better World.* Ethics International Press.

Tavanti, M. (2024). *Sustainability leadership: Theories, paradigms, and practices for emerging value-leaders.* Planet Healing Press.

Tiburi, M. (2021). *The Psycho-Cultural Underpinnings of Everyday Fascism: Dialogue as Resistance.* Bloomsbury Publishing.

Tilly, C. (1992). *Coercion, capital, and European states, AD 990–1992.* Blackwell.

Tocqueville, A. de. 1994 [1835/1840]. *On Democracy in America.* Fontana Press.

Tolstoy, L. (1869). *War and Peace.* Penguin.

Traverso, E. (2019). *The New Faces of Fascism: Populism and the Far Right.* Verso Books.

Tscheschlok, B. (2024). *Tech Bro Messiahs: How Tech Billionaires are Spearheading Late-Stage Reactionary Politics.* Doctoral dissertation, University Honors College, Middle Tennessee State University.

Tufekci, Z. (2017). *Twitter and tear gas: The power and fragility of networked protest.* Yale University Press.

Twain, M. (n.d.). Attributed quote.

United Nations. (1945). *Charter of the United Nations and Statute of the International Court of Justice.* United Nations.

United Nations. (2005). *In larger freedom: Towards development, security and human rights for all.* United Nations General Assembly Report A/59/2005.

United Nations. (2021). *Our common agenda: A breakthrough for people and planet.* UN Publications.

United Nations. (2023). *Global Digital Compact: Shaping a shared digital future.* United Nations Digital Governance Report. https://www.un.org/en/summit-of-the-future/global-digital-compact

Vico, G. (1999). *The new science* (D. Marsh, Trans.). Penguin Classics. (Original work published 1744)

Vissing, Y. (2025). The Attack of Diversity, Equity and Inclusion (DEI) as an Attack on Human Rights Education. In: Zajda, J., Vissing, Y. (eds) *Globalisation, Human Rights and Education.* Globalisation, Comparative Education and Policy Research, vol 51. Springer.

Vosoughi, S., Roy, D., & Aral, S. (2018). The spread of true and false news online. *Science*, 359(6380), 1146-1151. https://doi.org/10.1126/science.aap9559

Weber, M. (1947). *The theory of social and economic organization.* Free Press.

Whitehead, A. L., & Perry, S. L. (2020). *Taking America Back for God: Christian Nationalism in the United States.* Oxford University Press.

Winters, J. A. (2011). *Oligarchy.* Cambridge University Press.

World Bank. (2023). *Financing climate action: The role of multilateral development banks.* World Bank Group.

Yiftachel, O. (2021). *Ethnocracy: Land, identity, and the politics of exclusion.* Stanford University Press.

Zakaria, F. (2021). *Ten lessons for a post-pandemic world*. W. W. Norton & Company.

Zakaria, F. (2007). *The Future of Freedom: Illiberal Democracy at Home and Abroad*. W.W. Norton & Company.

Žižek, S. (2012). Living in the Time of Monsters. *Counterpoints*, 422, 32–44. http://www.jstor.org/stable/42981752

Zuboff, S. (2019). *The Age of Surveillance Capitalism: The Fight for a Human Future at the New Frontier of Power*. PublicAffairs.

Zürn, M. (2022). *The politics of international authority: The rise of multilateralism*. Cambridge University Press.

Zürn, M. (2024). A Conclusion: The American Version of the Liberal Script, or How Exceptionalism Leads to Exceptionalism. In Börzel, T. A., Risse, T., Anderson, S. B., & Garrison, J. A. (Eds). *Polarization and Deep Contestations: the Liberal Script in the United States* (pp. 247-267). Oxford: Oxford University Press.

APPENDIX 1:

GLOSSARY

Anarchism: A political philosophy that advocates for the abolition of all forms of hierarchical authority, including the state, in favor of a self-managed, stateless society based on voluntary cooperation.

Anti-capitalism: Opposition to capitalism, often calling for systems that eliminate profit motives, class hierarchies, and economic exploitation. Anti-fascist movements may support anti-capitalist ideals in opposition to corporate and state-driven authoritarianism.

Anti-communism: Opposition to communism, often associated with fascist regimes that view communist ideology as a threat to nationalist or authoritarian rule.

Anti-immigration: Policies or beliefs opposing immigration, often on nationalist or xenophobic grounds. Anti-immigration is common in fascist ideologies, which may promote cultural or racial purity.

Anti-Marxism: Opposition to Marxist ideology, which advocates for class struggle and a classless society. Fascist regimes typically oppose Marxism, viewing it as a threat to the social order they enforce.

Anti-parliamentarianism: Rejection of parliamentary or representative democratic systems, favoring authoritarian rule or a single-party state as more efficient or direct.

Antifa: Short for "anti-fascist," a movement that opposes fascist, far-right, and white supremacist ideologies. Antifa advocates for direct action, including protests and resistance, to combat fascism and protect marginalized communities.

Authoritarianism: A leadership style emphasizing strict obedience to authority, often at the expense of personal freedoms. Authoritarian regimes centralize power and suppress opposition.

Chauvinism: Extreme patriotism and nationalism, often with a belief in national or racial superiority. Chauvinism is a trait commonly associated with fascist ideologies.

Civil Disobedience: A nonviolent form of protest against unjust laws or policies. Anti-fascist leadership may advocate for civil disobedience as a way to resist authoritarian control.

Collectivism: The prioritization of the group or nation over individual needs or desires. In fascist leadership, collectivism is often emphasized to strengthen unity and diminish individual rights.

Communism: A political and economic ideology that advocates for a classless society in which property and resources are communally owned. In contrast to fascism, communism seeks to eliminate class hierarchies and empower the working class.

Conservatism: A political philosophy that emphasizes tradition, social stability, and preservation of established institutions. While not inherently fascist, extreme conservatism can align with authoritarian ideologies when it opposes democratic or progressive reforms.

Corporatism: A system where economic and political power is distributed through corporate groups, such as business, labor, and military entities. Fascist regimes often employ corporatism to consolidate control and suppress opposition.

Counter-Narrative: An alternative perspective that challenges dominant ideologies, often used in anti-fascist education to dismantle propaganda and promote independent thought.

Critical Thinking: The ability to analyze and evaluate information objectively. Anti-fascist education promotes critical thinking as a tool for challenging propaganda and authoritarian narratives.

Cult of Personality: A form of hero-worship built around a leader, often used in fascist regimes to elevate the leader's image and suppress criticism by portraying them as infallible or superhuman.

Democracy: A system of governance where power is vested in the people, typically through elected representatives. Anti-fascist leadership seeks to protect and strengthen democratic institutions.

Dissent: Expression of opinions that differ from those in power. Dissent is a core element in anti-fascist leadership, which values freedom of speech and encourages questioning authority.

Egalitarianism: A belief in equality among people, often opposing social hierarchies. Anti-fascist ideologies support egalitarianism as a counter to fascist elitism and inequality.

Empathy: The ability to understand and share the feelings of others. Anti-fascist leadership emphasizes empathy, valuing the protection and dignity of all individuals.

Ethnic Nationalism: Nationalism based on shared ethnicity, culture, and heritage, often used to exclude minority groups. Fascist regimes frequently promote ethnic nationalism as a unifying, exclusionary identity.

Eugenics: A pseudo-scientific belief in improving human populations through selective breeding. Eugenics has been used by fascist regimes to justify racial hierarchies and oppressive policies.

Freedom of Expression: The right to voice one's opinions publicly without fear of retaliation. Anti-fascist leadership defends this freedom as a safeguard against authoritarianism.

Grassroots Activism: A bottom-up approach to social and political action, relying on the engagement of ordinary people rather than leaders alone. Grassroots activism is central to anti-fascist movements.

Heroism: The qualities of courage and bravery, often glorified in fascist ideologies as an ideal of strength and sacrifice for the nation.

Hierarchy: A system of ranks or levels within an organization or society. Fascist ideologies often promote strict hierarchical structures as a means of enforcing order and obedience.

Human Rights: Fundamental rights and freedoms entitled to all individuals. Anti-fascist leaders strive to uphold human rights in opposition to fascist repression.

Inclusive Education: An educational approach that promotes diversity and equality, aiming to empower marginalized groups. Anti-fascist leaders endorse inclusive education to counter fascist indoctrination.

Indoctrination: The process of teaching a person or group to accept a set of beliefs uncritically. Fascist regimes often use indoctrination to reinforce loyalty and suppress dissent.

Liberalism: A political ideology that values individual rights, freedoms, and equal opportunities. Anti-fascist ideologies often align with liberalism's emphasis on democracy and civil liberties.

Machismo: An exaggerated masculinity or belief in male dominance, often associated with fascist and authoritarian values.

Marxism: A socio-political theory developed by Karl Marx that advocates for the working class's empowerment and a classless society. Marxism is opposed to fascism's hierarchical and nationalist tendencies.

Masculinity: Qualities traditionally associated with men, which fascist ideologies often glorify as strength, dominance, and aggression.

Militarism: The glorification of military power and values, which fascist leaders use to create a unified, disciplined society ready for conflict or expansion.

Nativism: Favoritism toward native-born citizens over immigrants, often associated with anti-immigrant and xenophobic policies in fascist ideologies.

Nationalism: In fascist contexts, an extreme form of patriotism that promotes the superiority of one nation or race, often used to justify exclusion or aggression toward others.

Natural Law: A philosophical belief in inherent moral principles governing human behavior. Fascist ideologies may misuse natural law to justify rigid hierarchies or social order.

Neo-Colonialism: The practice of using economic, political, or cultural pressures to control or influence other countries, often in exploitative ways. Anti-fascist leaders may oppose neo-colonial practices as a form of modern oppression.

Neoliberalism: A modern economic approach that emphasizes free-market capitalism, deregulation, and reduced government intervention. Anti-fascist ideologies may critique neoliberalism when it leads to economic inequality or corporate dominance.

One-Party State: A political system where a single political party controls the government, often suppressing opposition. Fascist regimes often establish one-party states to consolidate power.

Oppression: Systematic, unjust treatment or control of people, often based on race, class, gender, or political affiliation. Fascist regimes use oppression to maintain order and discourage opposition.

Persecution: Harsh treatment or hostility toward individuals or groups, especially due to political or ideological beliefs. Fascist leadership employs persecution to eliminate perceived threats.

Pluralism: A political philosophy that values diversity in political and social thought, allowing multiple groups to coexist. Anti-fascist ideologies support pluralism as an antidote to totalitarian control.

Populism: Political approach aimed at appealing to the interests and emotions of the general population, often by promoting a division between "the people" and the elite. Populism in fascist regimes may be used to galvanize support by scapegoating outsiders.

Protectionism: Economic policies aimed at shielding a country's industries from foreign competition. Fascist regimes often use protectionism to support nationalistic economic goals.

Racism: Discrimination or prejudice based on race. Fascist ideologies often promote racist beliefs to justify social hierarchies and exclusionary policies.

Resistance: Organized efforts to oppose oppression, authoritarianism, or injustice. Anti-fascist leaders encourage resistance as a form of defending freedom and democratic values.

Scapegoating: Blaming a person or group for societal problems. Fascist leaders use scapegoating to create unity against a common "enemy" and distract from their own failings.

Social Darwinism: A belief in the survival of the fittest within societies, often used by fascist leaders to justify inequality and racial hierarchies.

Social Interventionism: The belief in government intervention to address social issues. Anti-fascist ideologies may support interventionism to prevent inequality and protect marginalized groups.

Social Justice: The concept of fairness and equality within society, often in relation to rights and resources. Anti-fascist leaders advocate for social justice as a means to counteract oppression.

Socialism: An economic and political system advocating for shared ownership of resources and means of production. Anti-fascist ideologies often align with socialist principles to promote social equality and reduce authoritarian control.

Solidarity: Unity and support within a group working toward a common goal. Anti-fascist movements emphasize solidarity as a strategy for collective resistance.

State Capitalism: An economic system in which the state has significant control over businesses and resources. Fascist regimes may use state capitalism to enforce nationalistic goals and strengthen state power.

Supercapitalism: An extreme form of capitalism where corporate interests dominate and influence government policy, often leading to inequality. Anti-fascist ideologies critique supercapitalism for undermining democracy.

Surveillance State: A government that extensively monitors its citizens, often justified as necessary for national security. Fascist regimes employ surveillance to maintain control and suppress dissent.

Syncretic Politics: The blending of political ideologies, often combining elements from opposite ends of the spectrum. Some fascist ideologies use syncretism to create hybrid systems to appeal to broader audiences.

Third Position: A political philosophy rejecting both capitalism and communism, often advocating for a blend of nationalism and socialism. Third Position ideologies can align with fascist views on national unity.

Totalitarianism: An extreme form of authoritarianism where the state seeks to control all aspects of public and private life, using propaganda, surveillance, and intimidation to maintain power.

Transformative Leadership: Leadership that aims to inspire change by empowering individuals and communities. Anti-fascist leaders prioritize transformative leadership to create positive societal change.

Tyranny: Oppressive and unjust use of power. Fascist regimes are often described as tyrannical, seeking to control citizens' lives through fear and force.

Ultranationalism: Extreme nationalism that promotes aggressive loyalty to the nation, often at the expense of other nations or ethnic groups. Fascist ideologies often include ultranationalism to justify militarism and expansion.

White Nationalism: A form of nationalism based on the belief that white people should maintain a dominant position in society. Fascist ideologies frequently promote white nationalism to reinforce racial hierarchies.

White Supremacy: The belief that white people are superior to other races. White supremacy is a core tenet in many fascist ideologies, used to justify discrimination and exclusion.

Xenophobia: Fear or hatred of foreigners or outsiders, often exploited by fascist leaders to unify citizens against perceived external threats.

APPENDIX 2:

ANNOTATED BIBLIOGRAPHY

PART 1: FOUNDATIONAL WORKS ON FASCISM AND TOTALITARIANISM

The Authoritarian Personality – Theodor W. Adorno et al. (1950): This seminal study explores the psychological foundations of authoritarianism and fascism. Adorno and his colleagues identify personality traits—such as rigid adherence to conventional norms and submissiveness to authority—that make individuals more susceptible to fascist ideologies. Their research underscores how psychological dispositions and early socialization shape authoritarian tendencies, helping subsequent scholars analyze the interplay between personality, political beliefs, conformity, and prejudice.

The Origins of Totalitarianism – Hannah Arendt (1951): Arendt's classic work investigates the conditions that give rise to totalitarian regimes, including anti-Semitism, statelessness, and the breakdown of class structures. She distinguishes totalitarianism from other forms of authoritarianism, showing how mass movements and ideology enable total control. This book remains a crucial reference for understanding the structural and ideological mechanisms that foster fascism and authoritarianism.

Fascism: What It Is and How to Fight It – Leon Trotsky (1930s): Trotsky presents fascism as a mass movement mobilized to protect capitalist structures by crushing the working class. He argues for a unified, organized socialist resistance to dismantle fascist power structures. His work remains relevant to contemporary anti-fascist movements emphasizing class consciousness, worker solidarity, and strategic resistance.

Fascism and Democracy – George Orwell: Orwell examines the dangers of fascism and the fragile nature of democracy. His analysis highlights how propaganda, state control, and public manipulation erode democratic systems, emphasizing the necessity of free thought and civic engagement to counter authoritarianism.

PART 2: HISTORICAL AND ANALYTICAL STUDIES ON FASCISM

The Anatomy of Fascism – Robert O. Paxton (2005): Paxton dissects fascism not as a fixed ideology but as a political process that exploits crises to gain legitimacy. He explores how fascist movements appeal to national unity, manipulate emotions, and use violence to consolidate power. His rigorous historical analysis makes this work essential for understanding how fascism emerges and evolves.

Fascism: A Warning – Madeleine Albright (2018): Albright, a former U.S. Secretary of State, provides a historical and personal analysis of fascism, warning of its resurgence in contemporary politics. She highlights characteristics of fascist leaders—such as charismatic authoritarianism, nationalism, and fear-based manipulation—while offering strategies for defending democratic institutions.

How Fascism Works: The Politics of Us and Them – Jason Stanley (2018): Stanley explores the linguistic and ideological tactics of fascist leaders, identifying ten pillars of fascist politics, such as mythic past glorification, anti-intellectualism, and propaganda. His work bridges historical analysis and contemporary concerns, offering insights into how fascist rhetoric seeps into public discourse and policymaking.

Erasing History: How Fascists Rewrite the Past to Control the Future – Jason Stanley (2024): Stanley examines how fascist regimes distort historical events to legitimize their power and weaken public resistance. He argues that rewriting history is a crucial strategy for authoritarian control, making the preservation of accurate historical narratives essential for democratic resilience.

PART 3: CONTEMPORARY AUTHORITARIANISM AND RESISTANCE

Autocracy, Inc.: The Dictators Who Want to Run the World – Anne Applebaum (2024): Applebaum examines how modern autocracies—from Russia to Hungary—collaborate to undermine democratic norms, using media manipulation, corruption, and coercion to sustain their power. She highlights the global networks that allow authoritarian regimes to reinforce one another, providing crucial insights for contemporary anti-fascist strategies.

Strongmen: Mussolini to the Present – Ruth Ben-Ghiat (2020): Ben-Ghiat traces the evolution of authoritarian leadership, analyzing figures like Mussolini, Gaddafi, and Putin. She explores how these leaders cultivate loyalty, spread fear, and manipulate populist narratives to maintain control. Her work is invaluable for recognizing the patterns of fascist and authoritarian leadership.

From Fascism to Populism in History – Federico Finchelstein (2019): Finchelstein traces the ideological and historical evolution of fascism and populism, examining their intersections and critical distinctions across the 20th and 21st centuries. Through a comparative and transnational lens, he explores how authoritarian movements—from European fascism to modern populist regimes—employ rhetoric, leadership styles, and institutional strategies to reshape democratic culture. By analyzing figures like Trump, Chávez, Perón, Duterte, and Le Pen, Finchelstein challenges simplistic labels and provides a nuanced framework for understanding the shifting boundaries between authoritarianism and populist democracy. The work offers crucial insights into the fragility of democratic norms in the face of charismatic, polarizing leadership.

Me the People: How Populism Transforms Democracy – Nadia Urbinati (2019): Urbinati offers a rigorous and timely analysis of populism as a distinct and transformative form of representative democracy. Rather than dismissing populism as merely anti-democratic, she argues that it reconfigures democratic principles by fostering a direct, unmediated relationship between the leader and a selectively defined "people." By sidelining political parties, independent media, and pluralistic representation, populist leaders claim exclusive legitimacy while marginalizing dissenting voices. Urbinati distinguishes populism from classical authoritarianism and fascism, yet warns of its potential to erode constitutional norms and democratic checks. Blending political theory with contemporary case studies, the book provides a critical framework for understanding how populism reshapes governance and threatens democratic resilience.

PART 4: ANTI-FASCIST STRATEGIES AND EDUCATION

On Tyranny: Twenty Lessons from the Twentieth Century – Timothy Snyder (2017): Snyder distills lessons from 20th-century fascist regimes into twenty actionable steps for resisting authoritarianism. He emphasizes defending institutions, recognizing propaganda, and standing against oppression, making this book a practical guide for democratic resistance. These themes are further developed in his follow-up, *On Freedom* (2024), where Snyder deepens his reflection on the responsibilities of democratic citizenship, exploring how truth, history, and civic courage are essential to preserving freedom in an age of rising authoritarian threats.

Antifa: The Antifascist Handbook – Mark Bray (2017): Bray provides a historical overview of anti-fascist movements, detailing their tactics, successes, and controversies. He argues for a proactive stance against fascism and examines the effectiveness of direct action strategies in countering authoritarian threats.

Anti-Fascism: The Course of a Crusade – Paul Gottfried (2021): Gottfried critiques modern anti-fascist movements, questioning their methods and the broad application of the "fascist" label. He explores how anti-fascism can sometimes stifle legitimate political discourse, sparking debate on the boundaries of anti-fascist activism.

Teaching Anti-Fascism: A Critical Multicultural Pedagogy for Civic Engagement – Michael Vavrus (2022): Vavrus focuses on education as a tool for resisting fascism, offering a pedagogical framework that fosters critical thinking, inclusivity, and civic engagement. His work highlights the role of educators in cultivating democratic resilience and preparing students to challenge authoritarianism.

How to Stop Fascism: History, Ideology, Resistance – Paul Mason (2021): Mason offers a forceful and urgent analysis of the resurgence of fascism in the 21st century, linking contemporary authoritarian movements to the ideological, economic, and psychological roots of historical fascism. Drawing on global examples—from Europe to Brazil, India, and Turkey—he argues that fascism is a recurring response to capitalist crisis, marked by nationalism, violence, and the suppression of democratic values. Combining historical insight with activist energy, Mason lays out a radical and hopeful blueprint for resisting the far right through civic engagement, democratic solidarity, and economic justice. The book serves both as a warning and a call to action, challenging readers to confront authoritarianism with clarity and courage.

PART 5: TECHNOCRACY AND CORPORATE POWER

Technocracy: The New American Corporate Monarchy – Richard Bachmann (2025): Bachmann examines how corporate and technological elites wield unchecked power, shaping public policy and economic systems to serve their interests. He argues that technocratic governance, if left unchallenged, threatens democratic accountability and public autonomy. His work provides a critical analysis of the modern convergence of economic, technological, and political power structures, offering insights into how corporate technocracy erodes democratic decision-making.

The Big Nine: How the Tech Titans & Their Thinking Machines Could Warp Humanity – Amy Webb (2020). Webb explores the outsized influence of nine major tech corporations—based in the U.S. and China—on global governance, economy, and social structures. She warns of the increasing power of AI-driven decision-making in shaping public policy, labor markets, and even individual autonomy. Webb's book is essential for understanding the geopolitical and ethical implications of unchecked technological dominance.

The Age of Surveillance Capitalism: The Fight for a Human Future at the New Frontier of Power – Shoshana Zuboff (2020): Zuboff's groundbreaking work exposes how tech corporations manipulate behavioral data to consolidate economic and political power. She argues that surveillance capitalism—where personal data is commodified and used to predict and influence behavior—threatens democracy, autonomy, and human rights. This book is critical for analyzing how corporate technocracy operates through data extraction and algorithmic control.

The Technology Trap: Capital, Labor, and Power in the Age of Automation. United Kingdom: Princeton University Press – Carl Benedikt Frey (2020): Frey explores how advances in AI and automation are accelerating a shift toward technocratic governance, where power resides increasingly with experts, algorithms, and data-driven decision systems rather than elected representatives. He analyzes historical and contemporary patterns showing how technological progress can undermine democratic institutions by concentrating authority in the hands of technical elites. The book serves as a cautionary study on the erosion of democratic agency in favor of technocratic rule, urging a reevaluation of how societies integrate technology with governance.

Democracy Hacked: How Technology is Destabilising Global Politics – Martin Moore (2018): Moore investigates how digital technologies are being weaponized to undermine democratic systems worldwide. He examines the rise of information warfare, data mining, microtargeting, and algorithmic manipulation by authoritarian states, political operatives, and corporate elites. The book exposes the vulnerabilities of digital infrastructure and social media platforms, showing how they are exploited to distort public opinion, spread disinformation, and erode civic trust. Moore calls for urgent democratic reforms to safeguard electoral integrity and rebuild the democratic process in an era increasingly shaped by surveillance, polarization, and technological manipulation.

APPENDIX 3:

GCQ ASSESSMENT

Assessment: Governance Classification Questionnaire (GCQ)

Author: Marco Tavanti (2025)

Application: This resource is freely available for non-profit educational use with proper attribution.

GCQ Introduction

The Governance Classification Questionnaire (GCQ) is a diagnostic tool for analyzing leadership styles across various governance models. Whether you're assessing a political figure, corporate executive, or institutional authority, this questionnaire helps you evaluate how leadership decisions impact democratic principles and power dynamics.

By responding to questions on elections, opposition, media, civil liberties, economic policies, and more, you'll identify where a leader falls on a spectrum—from Liberal Democracy to Fascism—with categories like Technocratic Oligarchy and Populist Authoritarianism in between. This framework is not about rigid labels but about recognizing patterns and assessing how leaders strengthen or undermine accountability.

After completing the questionnaire, tally your responses to determine the dominant governance type. Keep in mind that leaders often exhibit traits from multiple models, especially during crises or transitions.

Designed for students, analysts, and engaged citizens, the GCQ promotes critical reflection on how power is exercised, how institutions evolve, and how to spot early signs of democratic backsliding. Use it as a foundation for deeper analysis, discussion, and action toward more accountable and inclusive governance.

GCQ Instrument

1. How does the leader respond to political opposition?
  A. Encourages open debate and respects dissenting views.
  B. Seeks input from experts and ignores unqualified opposition.
  C. Undermines critics but allows controlled opposition.
  D. Calls critics "enemies" and stirs public anger against them.
  E. Eliminates opposition through corruption, legal threats, or coercion.
  F. Uses violence or police/military force to crush all dissent.

2. How does the leader handle elections?
  A. Ensures free and fair elections with independent oversight.
  B. Supports elections but believes governance should be led by experts.
  C. Holds elections but manipulates media and institutions to favor the ruling party.
  D. Claims elections are rigged if they don't win; undermines legitimacy of results.
  E. Controls elections through elite influence, voter suppression, or legal loopholes.
  F. Abolishes elections or holds sham elections with no real opposition.

3. How does the leader engage with the judiciary?
  A. Respects judicial independence and rule of law.
  B. Prefers legal decisions made by expert panels or technocrats.
  C. Interferes in judicial decisions to favor government policies.
  D. Uses the judiciary as a political weapon against opponents.
  E. Places loyal judges in courts to protect elites and political allies.
  F. Completely dismantles or purges the judiciary to ensure total control.

4. How does the leader treat the media?
  A. Encourages free and independent press.
  B. Prefers media controlled by intellectuals, experts, or government.
  C. Limits press freedom through selective censorship and propaganda.
  D. Regularly attacks the media and brands journalists as enemies.
  E. Uses the state or corporations to control the media narrative.
  F. Shuts down or nationalizes all independent media.

GCQ ASSESSMENT | 199

5. **What is the leader's economic approach?**
   A. Supports free-market policies with government regulations for fairness.
   B. Bases economic decisions on expert knowledge, automation, and AI.
   C. Uses economic policies to strengthen state power and reward loyalists.
   D. Uses the economy as a tool for nationalism and punishes critics with economic retaliation.
   E. Concentrates wealth in the hands of the elite while suppressing economic mobility.
   F. Nationalizes industries and enforces state-controlled economies.

6. **How does the leader treat civil liberties?**
   A. Protects freedom of speech, assembly, and human rights.
   B. Values efficiency over individual liberties but does not suppress them.
   C. Restricts certain freedoms in the name of stability or national values.
   D. Uses patriotism and fear to justify limits on civil liberties.
   E. Criminalizes activism, whistleblowers, and civil rights groups.
   F. Completely abolishes civil liberties and enforces obedience.

7. **How does the leader handle national identity and minorities?**
   A. Promotes multiculturalism and equal rights.
   B. Sees national identity as secondary to economic or technological progress.
   C. Encourages nationalism but avoids direct discrimination.
   D. Promotes "us vs. them" rhetoric, scapegoating minorities.
   E. Enforces loyalty and excludes outsiders from power structures.
   F. Ethnically or ideologically purges minorities from society.

GCQ Scoring & Interpretation
- Count how many times you selected each letter (A–F).
- Your leader's dominant governance type is the one with the highest score.

GCQ Results
- **Mostly A's → Liberal Democracy**: Your leader operates within an open, pluralistic democracy with institutional checks and balances.
- **Mostly B's → Technocratic Oligarchy**: Your leader values expertise and efficiency but may limit broad political participation.

- **Mostly C's → Illiberal Democracy**: Your leader holds elections but weakens democratic institutions and restricts freedoms.
- **Mostly D's → Populist Authoritarianism**: Your leader prioritizes nationalism and strongman politics while undermining dissent.
- **Mostly E's → Oligarchic Autocracy**: Your leader ensures elite control over governance, wealth, and institutions.
- **Mostly F's → Fascist:** Your leader exhibits characteristics of authoritarianism as in fascism.

APPENDIX 4

ARI ASSESSMENT

Assessment: Authoritarianism Risk Index (ARI)

Author: Marco Tavanti (2025)

Application: This resource is freely available for non-profit educational use with proper attribution.

ARI Introduction

The Authoritarianism Risk Index (ARI) is a diagnostic tool designed to help assess the warning signs of democratic erosion and authoritarian consolidation. Whether evaluating political leaders, governance structures, or corporate leadership, this checklist provides a structured way to analyze power concentration, suppression of dissent, and institutional manipulation.

The ARI is divided into six key dimensions: Media Control, Judiciary Manipulation, Election Interference, Civil Liberties Restrictions, Concentration of Power, and Corporate Governance Parallels. Each section contains five warning signs, increasing in severity from subtle democratic erosion to full authoritarian control. Use this checklist to identify risks in political systems, organizations, or corporate governance structures.

I. Media Control and Propaganda
1. Limits press access to government or corporate activities, restricting independent journalism.
2. Discredits media by calling reports "fake news" or attacking journalists personally.
3. Controls major news outlets through state ownership, regulatory pressure, or corporate influence.

4. Uses propaganda to manipulate public perception and drown out dissenting voices.
5. Shuts down or criminalizes independent media through legal action or force.

II. Judiciary Manipulation and Rule of Law Erosion
1. Undermines judicial independence by attacking courts or judges who rule against them.
2. Appoints loyalists to judicial positions, reducing checks and balances.
3. Uses courts as a political weapon to punish critics, opposition leaders, or whistleblowers.
4. Weakens judicial oversight by reducing the power of courts to review executive decisions.
5. Rewrites laws or dissolves courts to eliminate legal constraints on power.

III. Election Interference and Political Manipulation
1. Spreads misinformation to manipulate public opinion before elections.
2. Restricts opposition candidates through legal barriers, intimidation, or disqualification.
3. Controls electoral processes by limiting voter access, suppressing turnout, or manipulating ballots.
4. Rejects unfavorable election results or claims fraud without evidence.
5. Abolishes elections or holds sham elections with no real opposition.

IV. Restrictions on Civil Liberties and Dissent
1. Limits public protests through excessive policing, surveillance, or legal barriers.
2. Restricts NGOs and civil society organizations that advocate for human rights and democracy.
3. Criminalizes whistleblowers, activists, or journalists who expose government or corporate wrongdoing.
4. Expands mass surveillance to monitor and intimidate citizens.
5. Imposes emergency laws or martial law to justify indefinite repression.

V. Concentration of Power and Personalist Rule
1. Expands executive powers beyond constitutional or legal limits.
2. Bypasses legislative bodies through executive orders or decrees.

3. Purges internal dissenters from government or leadership structures.
4. Extends term limits or seeks to remain in power indefinitely.
5. Cultivates a personality cult where loyalty to the leader replaces institutional governance.

VI. Corporate Governance Parallels: Business as an Authoritarian Model

1. Suppresses internal criticism by discouraging whistleblowing or punishing dissent.
2. Eliminates boardroom opposition through buyouts, legal threats, or consolidating leadership roles.
3. Manipulates markets and regulations to weaken competition or secure government favoritism.
4. Controls workforce through coercion—limiting union rights, surveillance, or forced loyalty.
5. Engages in state-corporate collusion to influence laws, suppress opposition, and monopolize power.

ARI Scoring and Interpretation

0–5 Checks: Low risk – No significant authoritarian tendencies, but continued vigilance is important.

6–10 Checks: Moderate risk – Some early warning signs of democratic backsliding or governance manipulation.

11–15 Checks: High risk – Serious concerns about democratic erosion, authoritarian control, or unchecked power concentration.

16+ Checks: Critical risk – Active authoritarian consolidation, institutional breakdown, or full authoritarian rule.

ARI Discussion Questions & Prompts

I. **Media & Democracy:** Why is a free press essential for maintaining democracy? What are some real-world examples of media control leading to authoritarian shifts? How can societies resist media suppression while ensuring responsible journalism?

II. **Judicial Independence & Rule of Law:** What happens when the judiciary is no longer independent? How do leaders manipulate judicial systems to consolidate power? Can a democracy survive without a strong, impartial judiciary? Why or why not?

III. **Electoral Integrity & Authoritarianism:** What are the key indicators of fair and free elections? How does election interference contribute to democratic backsliding? What strategies can be used to protect electoral integrity in at-risk democracies?

IV. **Civil Liberties & Political Stability:** Why are civil liberties considered the foundation of democratic governance? What are some historical or contemporary examples of governments suppressing dissent? How do governments justify restricting freedoms, and how should societies respond?

V. **Power Concentration & Institutional Strength:** What risks arise when power is concentrated in a single leader rather than shared across institutions? How do checks and balances prevent authoritarianism, and what happens when they fail? Are there cases where centralized leadership has led to stability rather than oppression?

VI. **Authoritarianism in Corporate Leadership:** In what ways do authoritarian traits appear in corporate governance? How does unchecked corporate power impact democracy and society at large? Should corporations be held to the same transparency and accountability standards as governments? Why or why not?

INDEX

Acemoglu (Daron), 42, 54-55, 60
Africa, 25, 46, 48-49, 58, 60, 73;
　African American, xx; Pan
　African, 82; South Africa, 25,
　36
Albright (Madeleine), 12, 188
AI (Artificial Intelligence), xiv, 60;
　cyberocracy, 26; governance,
　100, 142; surveillance, 34, 56,
　60; human rights, 152
America (American), democracy,
　58; exceptionalism, 105;
　fascism, 102–104; first, 84;
　German, xix; great, xix, 47,
　75; Latin, xxiii, xxv, 25, 121;
　Native, xvi, 57; North, 35;
　Revolution, 57, 105
Anarchism (Anarchy), 29-30, 100,
　181
Antifa, 113, 192
Arendt (Hannah), 14, 110, 111, 124,
　163, 187
Authoritarianism, 7, 22, 25, 30,
　33, 78, 80, 123, 152, 158
Autocracy, 23, 24, 25, 30, 33
Berlusconi (Silvio), xxiv, 90, 91,
　92, 93, 94, 95

Bolsonaro (Jair), 30, 33, 36, 51, 67,
　83, 86, 87, 88, 89, 95
Bonhoeffer (Dietrich), 13, 111, 157,
　164
Brazil, 30, 36, 47, 67, 83, 86, 121,
　127
Business, 10, 64, 66, 125
California, 48, 151
Capitalism, 78, 116, 139, 140
Catholic, xxii, xxiii, 14, 18, 111,
　126, 132
Change, 47, 49, 69, 160
Chile, xi, 57, 82, 103, 104
China, 25, 26, 34, 56, 125, 141, 142
Christian, xxiv, 31, 83, 111, 131,
　132, 133, 146
Churchill, 11, 21, 110, 112
Civil, xx, 16, 17, 46, 48, 49, 57, 58,
　60, 67, 81, 111, 113
Communist, 50, 91, 96, 112
Comparing, 28, 77
Compromiser, 57, 58
Concentration, 23, 103
Control, 85, 92, 95
Corporate, xvii, 25, 64, 65
Corporatism, xvi, 27, 78, 81, 101,
　121, 182
Crisis, 65, 82, 84, 100

Cultural, 49, 50, 52, 67, 113, 124, 137
Cyberocracy, 26
Democracy, xii, xv, 16, 22, 25, 28, 29, 32, 33, 54, 82, 83, 85, 95, 145, 146, 147, 153, 158
Depression, 37, 44, 46, 58, 81, 115
Derbyshire (Denis, Ian), 27, 30
Development, 118, 151, 158
Digital, 26, 125, 146, 149, 152
Dissent, 130, 135
Duterte, 30, 83, 87, 143
Dynamics, xii, xxvi, xxvii, 4, 7, 31, 32, 64, 85, 95
Eatwell (Roger), xxi, 34, 76, 96
Economy, 116, 118, 120
Education, xiii, 88, 99, 116, 119, 121, 123, 126, 129, 130, 136, 153
Erdoğan (Recep Tayyip), 30, 44, 49, 50, 82, 85, 87, 94, 95, 96
Ethics, 102, 123, 125, 153
Eugenics 151, 183
Europe, xix, 35, 43, 49, 104, 115, 121, 132
Facebook, 144, 151
Fascism, xii, xxvii, 12, 23, 31, 33, 73-108
France, xxi, 24, 44, 47, 111, 112, 113, 115
Franco (Francisco), 31, 57, 81, 92, 97, 98, 103, 113, 116, 123
Freedom, 100
Freire (Paulo), 126, 127, 128, 129, 130
Fukuyama (Francis), 21, 42, 45, 55, 167
Gaddafi (Muammar), 82, 92

Gandhi (Mahatma), 13, 57, 68
Gentile (Giovanni), 14, 75, 76, 132
Germany, 29, 31-32, 37, 46, 49, 56, 60, 76, 78, 81, 85-89, 97-98, 109, 111-120, 124, 132, 140
Global, 58, 152
Governance, xxvi, Spectrum 21-39; Transformations 41-69, 142, 147, 150-152
Gramsci, xiii, xvi, 16, 18, 110
Gurr (Ted Robert), 25, 52
Habermas (Jürgen), 22, 29, 35
Hitler (Adolf), xix, 31, 37, 44, 46, 49, 50, 56, 67, 81, 82, 85, 86, 87, 90, 92, 103, 109, 111, 113, 116, 123, 132, 163
Hungary, 26, 30, 31, 33, 36, 44, 83, 87, 88
Huntington (Samuel), 24, 43, 61
Illiberal (Democracies), 22, 29, 31, 33, 36, 38, 83, 96
Illinois, xx, 6, 73, 170, 173-174
Indigenous, xxiv, 83, 87, 88
Industrial, 74, 118, 145, 146, 150
Inglehart (Ronald), 32, 34, 52
Institutions, 18, 23, 25, 32, 62, 126, 136
Intellectual, 17, 110, 111, 137
International, 47, 100, 117, 137, 152, 159
Italy, xvi-xxvi, 18, 25, 31, 73, 74, 75, 76, 79-81, 85-87, 91, 93, 97, 103, 109-116, 119-121, 126, 132, 135, 140-141
Japan, 25, 114-120, 139
Jewish, 88, 106, 112, 119
Justice, 9, 100, 101, 114, 125

INDEX | 207

King, 35, 48-49, 67, 81-82, 110, 138
Leadership, xii, xxvi, 3-20, 22, 30
Levitsky (Steven), 22-23, 26, 29-30, 33, 44, 147
LGBTQ+, 48, 50, 65, 83, 87, 100, 107
Lincoln (Abraham), 6, 11, 156
Machiavelli (Niccolò), xxii, 19, 53, 68
Machismo 100, 184
MAGA (Make America Great Again), 47, 51, 92
Mandela (Nelson), 44, 46, 48-49, 58, 60, 67, 157
Marty (Private), xix-xx
Media, 32, 95, 99, 123, 146, 147
Meloni (Giorgia), 49
Milani (Lorenzo), xiv, xxiii, xxvi, 14, 126, 127, 129-133, 135
Military, 24, 25, 56, 57, 119
Mindset, 32, 97, 99, 129, 134
Mobutu (Sese Seko), 26, 82, 92
Modi (Narendra), 30, 33, 87, 88, 94, 95, 96
Moral, 19, 53, 57, 102, 131, 134
Mounk (Yascha), 22, 30, 36, 96
Movement(s), xx, 46-52, 60, 67, 111, 136, 141
Mudde (Cas), 22, 30, 33, 36
Musk (Elon), 29, 32, 140, 141, 143
Mussolini (Benito), xvii, xix, 14, 16, 25, 31, 73-, 74-80, 85-98, 103, 109-110-119, 123, 127, 132, 140
Nationalism, 78
Nazi (Nazism), xix, xxi, xxii, xxiii, 12, 31, 46, 56, 67, 76, 78, 81, 85-89, 97-98, 103, 110-119, 124-125, 140, 160-161
Norris (Pippa), 32, 34, 52
North (Douglass), 24, 35, 42
Oligarchy, 22, 29, 33
Orbán (Viktor) 30, 33, 36, 44, 83, 87-88, 94-96
Orwell (George), xvii, 111, 124
Paxton (Roberto), 23, 31, 37, 74
Pertini (Sandro), xvi, 109, 110, 113, 114
Philippines, 30, 49, 83, 87, 143, 144
Pinochet (Augusto), xi, 57, 82, 92, 103-104
Plato, 15, 22
Policy, 100, 101, 151
Political, 12, 17, 21, 42, 52, 78, 87, 112, 120, 123, 136, 137, 152
Politics, 83, 85, 99
Populism (Populist), 22, 30, 33, 36, 84, 95-96
Power, 3-18, 23, 55, 103, 144
Putin (Vladimir), 30, 34, 37, 44, 57, 84-96, 103, 121
Racism 116, 125, 130, 185
Reagan, 12, 131
Republic, 22, 31, 43, 46, 53, 56, 81, 103, 109
Resistance, 7, 16-19, 110-113, 136-137
Ressa (Maria), 143, 144, 153
Revolution, 46, 49, 50, 57, 67, 82, 105, 145-146, 150
Rights, xx, 46-50, 60, 67, 101, 117, 161
Robinson (James), 42, 54, 163
Roman, xxii, 43, 56, 73, 175

Roosevelt (Eleanor), 161
Roosevelt (Franklin Delano), xvii, xxiv, 10, 110, 112, 160
Roosevelt (Theodore), 9, 13, 44, 58
Rovira Kaltwasser (Cristóbal), 22, 30, 33, 36
Rule, 22-26
Russia, 26, 30, 34, 37, 57, 84-85, 91, 103, 111, 113
Salvini (Matteo), 49
Sfeir-Younis (Alfredo), xii, 156, 159
Silicon (Valley), 29, 140-145, 154
Singapore, 25, 26, 29, 32, 35, 57
Smith (Adam), 53
Socialism 29, 38, 76-81, 113
Soviet Union, 24, 44, 50, 57, 61, 84, 132
Spain, 31, 81, 97, 103, 113, 116, 119-121, 132
Spanish, 57, 81, 111, 113
Stanley ((Jason), 85, 121
State-controlled, 117, 118, 147, 148
Surveillance, 100, 139, 140, 147, 149
Sustainability, xii, 6, 10, 13, 48, 101
Systems, 26, 27, 77, 116, 166

Tarrow (Sidney), 52
Tavanti (Marco), xxii, xxiii, xxiv, xxvii, 5, 15, 16, 20, 127, 156
Teaching, xxiii, 121, 123, 129
Technocracy, xii, 26, 139-144
Techno-fascism, 139-154
Technology, 55, 66, 100, 125, 146, 147
Thiel (Peter), 140, 142, 143, 144
Turkey (Republic - Türkiye Cumhuriyeti), 26, 30, 44, 49, 82
Twitter (X), 140-143, 152
United States, xvii, xxv, 26, 29, 35-36, 47-48, 60, 85, 104-105, 115, 151, 154
Universal, 117, 119, 148, 161
University, 126
Women, 48, 49, 67, 119
World War II (WWII), xv, ixx, xxi, 25, 50, 74, 108, 111, 113, 137, 159
Zakaria (Fareed), 22, 29, 36
Ziblatt (Daniel), 23, 30, 44, 147
Zuboff (Shoshana), 139, 140

ABOUT THE AUTHOR

Dr. Marco Tavanti is an Italian-born sociologist and professor of leadership and sustainability at the University of San Francisco's School of Management. Rooted in his family's history and shaped by decades of international work in social justice and sustainable development—including collaborations with the United Nations—he has cultivated a strong anti-fascist perspective and a deep commitment to ethical leadership.

As an advocate for critical education and conscious leadership, Dr. Tavanti's work bridges academia, policy, and practice to empower leaders across sectors. His research focuses on the intersections of democracy, governance, and sustainability, offering insights into how leadership can either uphold justice or enable authoritarianism.

His recent books include *Sustainability Beyond 2030* (Routledge, 2025), *Sustainability Leadership* (Planet Healing Press, 2024), *Sustainability Ethic*s (Ethics International Press, 2023), and *Developing Sustainability in Organizations* (Palgrave, 2023). *Decoding Leadership* reflects his lifelong commitment to examining power dynamics and equipping leaders with the tools to foster inclusive, just, and sustainable societies.

Learn more at www.marcotavanti.com

www.ingramcontent.com/pod-product-compliance
Lightning Source LLC
Chambersburg PA
CBHW020538030426
42337CB00013B/896